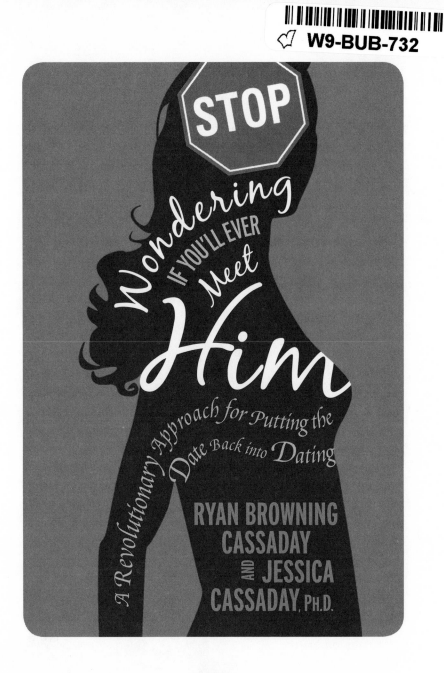

STOP

Wondering IF YOU'LL EVER Meet

Him

A Revolutionary Approach for Putting the Date Back into Dating

RYAN BROWNING CASSADAY AND JESSICA CASSADAY, PH.D.

HAY HOUSE

HAY HOUSE, INC.
Carlsbad, California • New York City
London • Sydney • Johannesburg
Vancouver • Hong Kong • New Delhi

Published and distributed in the United States by: Hay House, Inc.: www.hayhouse. com • *Published and distributed in Australia by:* Hay House Australia Pty. Ltd.: www.hayhouse.com.au • *Published and distributed in the United Kingdom by:* Hay House UK, Ltd.: www.hayhouse.co.uk • *Published and distributed in the Republic of South Africa by:* Hay House SA (Pty), Ltd.: www.hayhouse.co.za • *Distributed in Canada by:* Raincoast: www.raincoast.com • *Published in India by:* Hay House Publishers India: www.hayhouse.co.in

Editorial supervision: Jill Kramer   •   *Design:* Amy Rose Grigoriou

Library of Congress Cataloging-in-Publication Data

Cassaday, Ryan Browning.
  Stop wondering if you'll ever meet him : a revolutionary approach for putting the date back into dating / Ryan Browning Cassaday and Jessica Cassaday.
     p. cm.
  ISBN-13: 978-1-4019-1971-9 (tradepaper : alk. paper) 1. Dating (Social customs)--United States. 2. Single women--Life skills guides. I. Cassaday, Jessica. II. Title.
  HQ801.A5-Z.B867 2008
  646.7'7082--dc22
                                          2008014679

ISBN: 978-1-4019-1971-9

11 10 09 08   4 3 2 1
1st edition, October 2008

Printed in the United States of America

Hay House Titles of Related Interest

TO OUR LOVE,
AN UNEXPECTED ROMANCE
THAT TRANSFORMED OUR LIVES.

TO YOUR LOVE,
WHETHER PRESENT OR
SOON TO BE DISCOVERED.

AUTHORS' NOTE:

THE NAMES AND IDENTITIES
OF PEOPLE IN THIS BOOK
HAVE BEEN CHANGED
TO PROTECT THE PRIVACY
OF THE INDIVIDUALS.

Contents

Preface

You may be *wondering* what a married couple could teach you about dating. Maybe this story will help answer that question. . . .

Two people we know began to follow our revolutionary dating approach while they were working together. It started out innocently, as they were old friends who had gone into business together. Both of them were driven and optimistic about finding love in their lives, but they were also focused on their careers. Nonetheless, they followed our system, step-by-step, from first date to committed relationship.

His name is Ryan, and he's a life coach; her name is Jessica, and she's a psychologist.

Neither one of us expected to fall in love . . . and certainly not with each other! Life is funny when it comes to matters of the heart. When you are open and ready for love, unexpected possibilities will enter your life.

Introduction
Stop Wondering

Stop wondering if you'll ever meet him. Stop wondering this *minute*. Seriously . . . we mean it.

Stop it! Right now. You know what we're talking about here; you know all too well what's going on. In fact, you probably had your own idea of *him* the second you read the book title.

Maybe your "him" is the "One" or simply your dream man. He might be the guy who sits next to you at work or on the train in the morning. He could be in your college psych class or the single father at the PTA meeting with those gorgeous blue eyes. He may be someone you know, someone you've never met (but hope to soon), or someone you only meet each night in your dreams.

And then what happens if you do meet *him?* Now you must endure those agonizing moments in a developing relationship, wondering if there even *is* a relationship. This part of dating represents a state of being where you're consumed with questions about *where* he is when he isn't with you, *what* he's doing, and *who* else he might be doing it with (and is protection involved?). You may ask yourself, *Why hasn't he called? What is he thinking? What does he want? <u>Who</u> does he want . . . how can I make <u>him</u> want <u>me?!</u>*

🛑 Wondering . . .

You may have wondered many times about a man's reasons for not trying to get your phone number, not calling when he said he would, not asking you out again, or not wanting to commit—we could go on and on. Despite your (often) irrational fears, the truth is, there could be many plausible reasons that keep a perfectly good man *(him)* from doing any of the above.

For instance, why hasn't he called you?

At one time or another, you've probably thought of all the obvious excuses: asteroid attack; he was in a ten-car pileup on the way home and is muttering your name in the ICU (and obviously needs your help); your phone service is canceled and no one told you; the President needs his help with national security, but he's been thinking about you the whole time . . . right?

Look, we don't know *you* personally, and we don't know *him*. If we could pull him out of a hat and hand him to you, we would. Yet we know you're sitting there waiting for him (whoever he is) to materialize, reach out to contact you, and confirm that there's someone out there who's meant for you. Your feelings of wanting love are real, and men want love, too.

Now it's finally time for you to stop wondering if you'll ever meet him, because we're about to change everything for you starting with one word: *dating.* This book is about changing the way you find him, date him, and start a relationship with him so you don't squander real potential. In this hanging-out, hooking-up culture, we want to help you put the *date* back into dating so you can find the love that you want.

So will you ever meet *him?* Hey, we warned you: *Stop wondering.*

Seriously. We mean it!

Do You Know Julie?

Meet Julie, a 32-year-old advertising executive who decided to go prowling for cute guys on a Saturday night with her good friend Amanda, a 36-year-old high-school teacher.

The girls, as we'll call them, were Ready—capital *R* for romance. They had the professionally blown-out hair for $36 plus tip, stylish 7 jeans, the latest MAC makeup perfectly applied, and the ideal meet-greet-feel-the-heat place: a neighborhood block party. Thanks to Amanda's weak bladder, Julie found herself sitting alone on a lawn chair when Sam decided to make his move.

A 37-year-old lawyer at a top Chicago firm, Sam was on his way in life with his luxury condo and sleek black Beemer parked around the corner. Sam didn't give Julie a typical pickup line; he gave her something better—a promise that there are still great guys out there and that maybe she'd found *him*. What else could Julie think about a man this good-looking who made a beeline for her and said in a sweet voice, "Hey, I was looking over and saw you sitting here all alone. I had to come up and introduce myself."

They talked for 20 minutes and at the end of the conversation, Julie happily gave Sam her cell-phone number, home number, work number, e-mail, and how to reach her next of kin—kidding on that last part . . . well, almost. Let's just say that there was no way he could lose her number(s).

He didn't hesitate to use it and promptly called later that night and asked her out for the weekend! On Friday night, Julie found herself at a romantic Italian restaurant where she basically gazed across a red-checkered tablecloth at her handsome lawyer/future husband. God, how else could this fairy tale end?

And Sam didn't just bring a dozen long-stemmed red roses to the restaurant (which he actually did); he did something even more romantic: He *futured* her throughout the meal.

He said, "Do you like Maine? Someday it would be great for us to go there to see the fall leaves. I own this really amazing cabin with a wood-burning fireplace and an outdoor Jacuzzi. Really cozy and intimate."

As she listened, Julie was mentally picking out china patterns and children's names. She thought, *I love Maine! Well, I've never actually been there, but I love leaves, trees, and cuddling by the fireplace. And I certainly adore Jacuzzis!* Sam was obviously the One. She finally met *him!*

Her friend Amanda confirmed it during the absolutely mandatory two-hour, post-date, post-pasta phone call. Yes, Julie kissed him passionately before getting into a cab that night. He had great lips because, of course, her soul mate would come in one variety: perfect.

Boy meets girl, boy dates girl, and boy amazes girl. A few days after their first date, Sam called Julie out of the blue.

"I wanted to tell you that I had a fantastic time the other night," he said, "and I was wondering if you'd like to go boating with me on Saturday."

Another wonderful date culminated in some serious kissing. By the way, Julie was definitely not gonna give it up because she had a three-date rule, and she wasn't *that kind of girl*. But then the kissing got hot, and the moment felt so damn right. The boat was swaying, the sun was setting, and the champagne was so sweet and intoxicating. Why did he have to put Barry White on in the background? Those CDs should come with condoms.

We won't even write about what happened next. Use your imagination.

We can read your mind. It wasn't *that* wild.

Okay, it was pretty wild. Let's just say that Julie played Barry White all week as a tribute.

And then . . . Monday and Tuesday passed while Julie remained in her love haze. Totally elated is the only way to describe how she felt about Wednesday arriving. "Hump Day" was *love day*, and Sam was going to call because it was his pattern. After all, he'd called last week at exactly 7:12 P.M. on Wednesday and asked what her weekend plans were, so naturally she expected to speak to him soon. Julie spent the entire day on cloud nine, and her girlfriends were equally excited, because by now the circle of those who knew every detail about Sam had expanded to her friends Vickie, Sally, and Joyce. Everyone was in the loop and on the Sam bandwagon with a vengeance. Sam was their man—and he'd better not disappoint Julie or they'd kill him.

On Wednesday night, Julie rushed home, took a pee, gobbled down a Lean Cuisine, and waited until 7:12 P.M. came . . . and went. *WTF!*

By 7:45 she began to get a bit worried. Certainly he'd call her that night. Then she decided to "maybe" the situation. She figured that *maybe* his best friend got dumped and he needed to have a beer with him. *Maybe* his ultra-demanding boss made him fly on a red-eye to New York. *Maybe* he forgot to bring his cell phone on this business trip. Yes, she was sure that was what had happened.

At midnight she woke up Joyce, who fully understood the need for Julie's late-night breakdown. Joyce had called Julie two nights earlier at 4 A.M. for exactly the same reason, and the two shared their concerns about her guy, Chad. They consoled and advised each other over chocolate and Doritos. Joyce assured her that Sam would call the next night.

Thursday

Julie went to work the following day feeling dejected. She even rushed home from a movie with her girlfriends (where she was almost kicked out by the ushers for repeatedly checking her cell phone for messages).

By 9 P.M. that night there was still no call, and Julie began to worry whether Sam was okay. *Why wouldn't he call? Everything was so perfect. Oh no—did I forget to pay my cell-phone bill? Was the phone company cutting me off from Sam? No, Joyce called five minutes ago, and the phone worked just fine. Maybe I should send him a text message.*

It wasn't going to win a Pulitzer, but after a two-hour consultation with her other relationship adviser Sally (also currently heartbroken over a guy named Bill), she finally wrote to Sam: "Just wanted to check in and see how everything's going."

Julie thought she sounded confident—like she wasn't sweating it.

By 11 P.M., she wasn't just sweating it, she was frantic and decided it was time for a call. With shaking fingers, she called Sam, listened hard, and couldn't believe it when *his voice-mail message came on. WTF!*

For a split second, she couldn't decide whether to just hang up (and call again in 15 minutes) or leave a message. She went for the message to sound less needy and said, "Hi, Sam—it's Julie. I haven't heard from you, and I'm really worried." She listened to her message and thought she sounded vaguely hysterical.

She pressed number three to rerecord it: "Hey, Sam. It's Julie. Just calling to say hi. (Pause.) So, hi. (Pause.) That's about it."

She listened to that one and thought she sounded like she needed special-education speech courses. Ten minutes later, she was still rerecording the message and settled on: "Hi, Sam. It's Julie. Call me."

She didn't notice how hostile she sounded.

By 2 A.M., he hadn't called back, and her mind raced. Maybe he'd met a supermodel at that supposed "business dinner" he said he was attending this week. Maybe they were in bed right now doing . . . *no, no, no!*

She decided this was utterly ridiculous. He was probably just trying to play it cool, so she'd play it cool, too. She stayed up watching *Bridget Jones's Diary* on HBO. At 2:10 A.M., the phone rang and her heart soared, but it was her friend Jenna wanting to see if Sam had called yet. Julie finally fell into bed completely depressed.

Friday

Julie checked her text messages every ten minutes, looking at her cell phone about a trillion times. *Nothing.* She tried to distract herself with work but ended up calling her home phone about 15 times that day. *Nothing.* By Friday night, she was completely wigged-out.

She couldn't sleep or eat, and kept replaying their two dates over and over again in her mind. She was sweating, her heart was racing, and worst of all, she was sure her forehead was breaking out.

And then something amazing happened, and it was a sign that there was hope: At 2:31 A.M., her phone vibrated, which was conveniently on her pillow with her hand on it—better safe than miss a call.

Sam texted her cell and wrote: "Hey! Whaddaya doin'?"

Julie was overwhelmed with joy and immediately sat up in bed, turned on the light, smiled a huge giggling grin, and then not only saved the note (to relish this moment again later), but immediately dialed Sam. She got no answer.

Huh?

She hit redial, and as it rang, her heart started to beat faster. Now she was really confused because he'd just texted her! And then his voice mail picked up with the usual, annoying, soul-destroying *Hey, it's Sam*—Julie hung up. One minute later, she called again . . . no answer.

WTF! She didn't know what to do, and in her panic she sent him a text, saying, "Hey! You just texted me and I called you. Where did you go?"

No response.

What about their future trip to Maine? What had Sam really meant when he'd said, "I can't wait to settle down, move out of the city, and have a family"? What about the damn cabin!

She was horrified as she speed-dialed her girlfriends. None of them could console her because they were stunned. Her friend Vickie said, "All lawyers are jerks—just forget about him. I guess he's just not that into—"

Oh, yeah, scratch that one. That's another book.

Julie was acting like an addict who needed her fix. After a long and lonely weekend, she approached Monday with renewed purpose. At lunch, she took a cab across town to eat at the hamburger joint Sam mentioned he ate at every day. Her plan was to innocently "just run into him." She arrived with such poise and was shattered after a quick glance around the room revealed there was no Sam.

An anxious week without Sam finally passed, and it was Friday night once more. Julie raced home because she figured that she'd waited long enough to call Sam again, and she was going to give it another try to see if he'd be around over the weekend.

She paused and focused herself before calling. This time she decided to say with false confidence, "Hi, it's Julie. Hope you had a great week; talk to you soon." She turned on the TV to distract herself afterward, and this time Sam texted back!

"Hey! What are you doing? Sorry I've been out of touch. Really want to see you. Are you free? Can I come over?"

Out of her mind thrilled, Julie knew that she had to compose herself because she didn't want to appear needy, so she waited *five whole minutes* and wrote back: "Oh, just got home." Visions of "the rules" danced through her head while she typed: "Get together? Why not?" She was proud that she didn't sound too anxious.

Sam arrived at 2 A.M., half drunk, but with what looked like love in his eyes. Julie was overwhelmed and knew that if he just spent one more night with her, then the two-story dream house in the burbs and the trip to Maine would surely become her reality. Certainly he'd realize that their chemistry and connection was better than anything else he'd experienced, and he'd know that she was the One.

If the sex was great, she knew that Sam would commit.

Julie fought her urge to ask too many questions about the last nine days (not that she was still counting) while they passionately hooked up. She even had a secret *Cosmo* trick where she twisted—okay, we'll stop again.

At 4 A.M., Sam stood by the side of her bed and gathered his clothes. Julie was shocked that he wasn't just going to use the john. Pulling on his Calvins, he smiled at her while fishing around in the dark to find his car keys. She couldn't believe it.

"Where are you going?" she blurted out, with fear in her voice that she couldn't even mask in the dark.

"Oh, Jules, sorry, but I've gotta train tomorrow morning for the marathon, and I don't have my stuff here. I had a great time, but it doesn't make sense for me to stay over," he quickly replied, blowing her a quick kiss as he stumbled down the hallway.

"I'll call ya later," he said.

Sam never called again.

Many of you know Julie; many of you have dated Sam.

He's Not the Problem

We know that on the surface this looks like another case of "What a jerk." Boy meets girl, girl falls hard for boy, and boy breaks girl's heart. However, that's not the whole story here.

Consider for a moment that Sam isn't necessarily a jerk.

Let's look at it through another lens and see it as an example of how critical missteps and a few wrong turns during the initial dating process can turn very real feelings of potential love into heartbreak. With a more effective dating approach—rather than just following what feels good in the moment—things could have been different for Julie.

Julie is like most women out there in that she's suffering while trying to meet a great guy. Whether or not your situation is similar to hers, you probably know how confusing and awkward dating can be these days.

Let's look back at Julie's story for a few moments. Remember when she was sweating it out about Sam calling? While she was stressing about him, she was actually perspiring, her pulse was racing, and her heart was pounding so hard that it felt as if there was a sledgehammer in her chest. The symptoms she felt aren't just exaggerations to make her situation seem more dramatic.

Her sweating, believe it or not, brings up an important point and perfectly illuminates our major discovery. It brings to light our observation that women in the modern dating environment all share similar *symptoms*. These physical manifestations weren't in Julie's imagination; they were really happening and, ultimately, negatively impacting her dating state of being.

MFDA

The manifestation of these symptoms is something we call *Modern Female Dating Anxiety* (MFDA). A "modern female" refers to any woman (of any age) in this current technological era, and "dating anxiety" refers to the distress (rapid pulse rate, pounding heart, and so on) brought on by an ambiguous dating process.

It's surprising to see that those who suffer MFDA symptoms are all, for the most part, confident women who are satisfied in almost every aspect of their lives: They have great friendships and careers, varied personal interests, and loving families—to name just a few winning areas of their lives. These modern females are able to lead dynamic lives and have numerous friends and colleagues, but when it comes to what we describe as the *Four Pillars of Intimacy*—dating, love, sex, and relationships—they all suffer from varying degrees of anxiety.

The remarkable thing about all these women (including you, perhaps) is that most are never paralyzed by anxiety in other areas of life. But when they date, they become nervous, uncertain, and feel out of control.

Sound familiar? We thought so, which is why we want to *end those feelings in you forever* as you read this book.

For over a decade, we've been researching dating trends, interviewing singles and couples, dating (yes, we've been in the trenches), documenting, and analyzing the complexities of the current dating environment in an attempt to understand how MFDA takes a perfectly grounded, reasonable woman and turns her into a total mess. This has been our mission—and our quest. It has taken us around the globe and now we're excited to announce that after speaking with thousands of women from all backgrounds and ages, we've finally figured out what's causing MFDA.

The problem isn't the guys you're dating or the city you live in. It's not *the one who got away* or that you're not pretty enough, have a few extra pounds, or feel too old. *The problem is that no one has ever taught you how to date.* This applies if you're single, divorced, widowed, or even if you're in a relationship and are wondering how to still "date" the man in your life.

In case the magnitude of what we just said was lost in the simplicity of the idea we just introduced, let us repeat it in another way: *No one formally taught you how to date!* You never attended a class; and there wasn't a best friend, older sibling, or cool parent who pulled you aside and taught you a dating method that you could rely on throughout the course of your life.

You're taught how to cross the street, do multiplication tables, drive a car, write a lit paper, run a business, fill out a tax return, and even how to straighten your hair with one of those ceramic tourmaline flat irons. But you were never taught how to date. You may have gathered some dating advice from your friends, the Internet, magazines, and movies that show and tell you how to flirt and even have mind-blowing sex, but no one ever explained a structured dating method to you that was designed to help you establish a deeply loving and committed romantic relationship.

We know that everyone wants to be loved and experience butterflies in the tummy. Believe us, we know that deep, passionate kissing is a wonderful experience to share with someone who turns you on. But if you don't know what you're doing while dating, then you might unknowingly skip over some key steps—like Julie and Sam did—which can squander or even extinguish relationship potential.

Do you want just a few of those kisses or a lifetime of them?

The key to genuine romance is to establish all Four Pillars of Intimacy: dating, love, sex, and relationships.

Dating is the initial means through which romantic potential is assessed. So when dealing with matters of the heart, you must be careful and wise in your dating decisions. When casually engaging in "hanging out and hooking up" dating behaviors, you're actually reducing your chances of love. That's right. Even when the moment feels so perfect, giving in to the passion without actually dating can ruin any long-term potential.

Do you desire intimacy and a connection with the man of your dreams? Do you want to satisfy that craving with lasting love? Are you already in a committed relationship but wish to ensure its longevity and make things even better? We believe that the most important things in life are love and happiness. Everybody wants these things. Then why is it so hard to find that love and hold on to it?

The purpose of this book is to answer these questions and show you how to eliminate MFDA from your life for good. Our revolutionary dating method will take the uncertainty out of the dating process, and it will give you a chance to forever change your romantic outcomes.

A Word about Us

As you may know, any good love affair starts with introductions, so consider this our first date. After all, who are we to be telling you how to find the love of your life?! Well . . . we'll tell you. . . .

Professionally, our students know us as Ryan and Dr. C, but as individual practitioners, we bring different things to the table.

A note from Ryan: Besides being the resident male point of view, I'm also a certified life coach. I consider myself to be a guide and consultant when it comes to discovering what you're looking for in life.

A note from Dr. C: I'm a licensed clinical psychologist, sex therapist, and expert when it comes to dating, love, sex, and relationships. I'm not just a clinician, but a modern female who spent many years in the dating trenches. I used the same approach we describe in this book to find, date, and marry *my "him."*

For over a decade, we've been developing the first and last dating approach you'll ever need. Naturally, you may wonder, *Why do I even need a dating method?* or better yet, *What does that even mean?*

Let's look at it this way: Without an effective dating method, you've come to rely on a lifetime of *haphazard* dating practices that have set you up to constantly endure MFDA. You've mapped into your personal history multiple occurrences of uncertainty and discomfort from a number of past situations that you carry with you into each new dating circumstance.

Your dating style has likely been like Julie's—filled with troubled love affairs and/or uncertainty. You've been keeping an internal (subconscious) log of all the negative experiences, and ultimately they continue to shape your choices and cause you to have trouble breaking these limiting dating patterns. This combo platter of experiences equals one huge helping of stress when it comes to romance.

You need a real method, because what you're doing now isn't working. We say this with complete understanding and absolutely no judgment. Remember, it's not your fault that no one taught you how to date. You can't be expected to know what you haven't learned. And aren't you sick of reading books that are fun but don't really provide lasting help? Aren't you even more disgusted with sitting home waiting for the phone to ring, bitching to girlfriends, and waking up alone?

A Dating School

In this book, we'll be taking you to a whole new kind of school. Yes, that's right—you're going back to class, but this time,

unlike the classes you took that didn't translate to real life, you'll finally take The Dating Class You *Wish* You Had. You'll learn things that will change your dating life from this point forward, and you'll cull information that will help you avoid future heartbreaks.

With this new dating method, you'll be on a journey where learning doesn't only involve a textbook, but just like the best part of grade school, you'll be taking a field trip. And you're headed to Nirvana: a place where the fruits of love are cultivated.

Along the way, we'll tell you more about Julie, whom you've previously met. We want to take a second and tell you a bit more about her before we continue. Since you're aware of some of her dating experience already, we want you to know the truth about her: "Julie" is a fictitious character we created to help tell the story of the dating crisis we spoke about earlier. She's actually a composite of our numerous clients and of anecdotes we've gathered from our surveys; everything that happens to her is a reflection of many common dating experiences that women have shared with us over the years.

Julie's stories are all *true,* and we've woven them into one tapestry to represent how common these situations are for thousands of modern female daters. Julie represents all of you out there—she is our *Everywoman.*

As Julie moves forward, we'll look at her experiences together to help you understand this groundbreaking approach to the dating process. We'll also give you quizzes, exercises, and a new vocabulary when it comes to romance, plus a cutting-edge way to reprogram your limiting thoughts and beliefs so that when you meet someone, you can truly explore the possibility for an intimate and lasting connection. By using our revolutionary dating system, you'll finally feel empowered and excited about dating— whether you're going on your first date or are jumping back into the dating pool after a breakup or divorce.

We can't wait for you to start practicing our innovative dating method, but if we were to just write out the six stages and then push you back into the pool, we'd be doing you a grave disservice.

Without getting to the root causes of your MFDA, we would only be providing a temporary fix to your dating anxiety. Our true intention is to help you tune in to your inner wisdom (not the "voice" of your MFDA), dissolve limiting beliefs, cultivate your own inner beauty, and finally find your ideal mate so that you can enjoy the lasting, fulfilling relationship you deserve.

We're making a big promise here, so please be patient with us (and keep reading!) as we carefully lay down the foundation (which makes up Part I of this book: "The Problem") and introduce our life-changing dating techniques (Part II: "Your Solution," which walks you through the process).

This is a whole new way of approaching a potential relationship. And when it comes to love, you'll *never* wonder again.

PART I

The Problem

Chapter 1

MFDA: A Dating Epidemic!

Let's start with the good news. It's important to acknowledge that it's not just women who have dating anxiety. I (Ryan) want to tell you that men have their own version of it—called MMDA (Modern Male Dating Anxiety)—and although it's different from what women experience, it's still equally distressing to a guy's dating process. Why am I telling you this? I just want you to know that you're not alone or at fault for having dating frustrations.

We (Ryan and Dr. C) are only addressing the female side of things because the reality is that men don't read dating books, while many women are smart and courageous enough to explore innovative solutions (like this one). Once more men realize that women are starting to date in this unique way, they'll need their own book, but for now, it's just the ladies and our favorite resident male, Ryan.

Okay, now that we've planted the seed in your mind, let's go back and visit our friend Julie for a few minutes. As we've explained, Julie represents the majority of women out there who admit that they've suffered quite a bit when it comes to dealing with matters of the heart. We've established the fact that dating tends to be

filled with ambiguity, confusion, and emotional pain. It's no wonder, then, that many modern female daters have come to expect these negative experiences when involved in potential relationship situations.

We know that you're independent, successful, driven, and capable of getting what you want in life (you're reading this book aren't you?). Modern females are sexually liberated and have the opportunity to be as extraordinarily successful as men. This means that you don't generally depend on a man to dictate the direction of your life, and you're capable of achieving anything you desire on your own. Yet, when it comes to men, the real question is: Why do they make you feel, think, and act so crazy?

Yes, we said it—*crazy*. But you're not crazy; it's the MFDA. In fact, you may be suffering from MFDA right now and not even consciously know it . . . although you probably *feel* it, don't you?

Let's look directly at *your* life for a moment. Have you ever met a guy you got really, really excited about only to have those sparks fizzle into frustration, confusion, hurt, or anxiety? If you said yes, then you've suffered from MFDA. Have you ever been so down-and-out about the idea of seeking a potential mate that you lost your desire to date? Again, it's your MFDA in action.

It's so simple, but even the small act of *wondering* if you'll ever meet him is one of the most familiar and recognizable symptoms of MFDA. You might have also wondered what he meant when he said those amazing things to you on your last date but hasn't called since—and you can't stop replaying the conversation in your head and are holding on to it desperately. Don't judge the situation; just see it for what it is while you're staring at the very quiet phone, wondering what his intentions were when he kissed you so passionately and then just disappeared from the planet. This is also MFDA.

Whether it's the simple act of wondering *if* you'll ever meet someone or *if* the guy you're currently "dating" will call you again, it's all MFDA. Another indication is when you're constantly feeling drained and frustrated. Is just the *idea* of dating a pain in the neck? If so, this reaction is (literally) due to the anxiety that is inspired in you by a confusing and often disappointing dating process.

For instance, have you ever wondered if you're even in a relationship with the guy you're sleeping with a few times a week? Are you really even dating, or are you just a fun "hook-up"? Are you questioning whether it was really a good idea to have sex with him on the second date? Wait . . . is casually hanging out at your apartment and having sex with him really even a *date?*

What is "dating" anyway—can it be defined? Does dating automatically involve sex? Is it casual, or does it always involve getting dressed up and going out to dinner? What if it doesn't work out with a guy you're seeing? Are you devastated afterward? Does it make you wonder if you'll ever find the right man or if you're cursed to lead a life saying, "Table for one, please"?

All of these questions (which will be dealt with in later chapters) contribute to your MFDA. In reality, the modern dating landscape can be frustrating to anyone who doesn't really know how to date—especially in an environment that has become even more complex with the introduction of the virtual world on the Internet. A whole new dating scene has emerged, and it's infused with all types of technology that can connect you to people around the world. With all these unfamiliar roads that are now available to you, how do you navigate intelligently and successfully? We'll show you how!

Do I Have MFDA?

Okay, it's quiz time. (We told you that you're going back to school!) The point of this is to determine if you, like Julie, have a case of MFDA.

Take a minute to think about how MFDA may exist in your life. Let's start with some questions:

1. When it comes to dating and relationships,
    do you have (or have you ever had):

    - Difficulty controlling anxious thoughts

    - Feelings of restlessness (being *on edge*)

    - Difficulty concentrating on anything
      but the guy

    - Mood swings or irritable feelings when
      you don't hear from him

    - Muscle tension, knots in your stomach,
      or neck pain

    - Trouble falling or staying asleep because
      you're agonizing over him

2. Do you feel apprehensive or uneasy before a date?

3. Do you constantly wonder how he feels about you?

4. Are you uncomfortable with the ambiguous dating
    process?

5. Do you become extraordinarily emotional or feel
    incredibly close to men you date only once or twice,
    but barely know?

6. When you're getting ready for a date (or are think-
    ing about an upcoming one), do you experience
    an increased pulse rate, butterflies in your stomach,
    or sweaty palms—even if you're a 34-year-old
    professional?

7. Do you doubt yourself or worry that you'll never
    meet *him?*

8. Do you wonder if you can cope with the complexities and uncertainties of all Four Pillars of Intimacy—especially the dating and relationship parts—and think that perhaps it's just easier to be single or get a cat?

If you answered yes to any of the above, don't worry, because you're not alone or strange. Your symptoms are *so* common—in fact, almost all women experience the exact same thing. No kidding. It doesn't matter how old you are or how many guys you've dated. If you're out there dating, you've encountered MFDA.

It's important to realize that everyone who's *ever* dated (including your friends, relatives, and even your favorite celebrities) has felt anxious, panicked, stressed out, or troubled at one time or another. In fact, one of the major ways in which women bond is by discussing their men, and hashing out the often-painful symptoms of MFDA.

So let's get to the root of the issue: Where does MFDA come from and what causes it?

What's Behind My MFDA?

Without any formal direction, you've created your own road map for intimacy. Every experience since the beginning of your dating life has contributed to your current knowledge about the Four Pillars of Intimacy. All of those collective moments have built on each other and charted a course through your romantic past, outlining (for you) how to date, what love looks like, and how to find it. Meanwhile, every failed relationship and broken heart that has fallen short of the storybook romance has taken its toll and chipped away at your otherwise reasonable and confident self. In

the absence of guidance and formal education, you're probably living in romantic survival mode.

It's time to stop surviving and start thriving!

Is it any wonder after a series of bad relationships and painful breakups that you're suffering from MFDA? You've come to expect hurt feelings and disappointment; thus, you're the sum total of your experiences. You may have met some good men along the way, but we're guessing that for the most part, you've fallen in many potholes and took some wrong turns.

Naturally, all this negativity affects your current dating life. When making romantic choices, you're inevitably drawing upon this internal reservoir of knowledge. If you've endured pain over and over, how can you fall in love again? You've likely shielded yourself from intimacy after a string of heartbreaks and troubling stories from your girlfriends who have been equally ravaged by the dating process. What methods, skills, or techniques can you use to help find *him,* date *him,* and have an intimate relationship with *him?*

Here's where we begin our class. First, you have to be able to observe MFDA in action. Recognizing it will help you learn to eliminate MFDA from your life for good. We want to show you the deep underbelly of this affliction so that you can eradicate this burden that's so profoundly affecting your dating success.

The Connection Between Dopamine and MFDA

Researcher and author Helen Fisher and her colleagues analyzed more than 3,000 brain scans of 18 recently lovestruck college students. The scans were taken while the students looked at a picture of their new love. Fisher expected the results to build on the previous findings of English researchers who completed a similar study of young men and women in love. When subjects were shown a photo of their romantic partner, their brain-activity pattern was markedly different from when they looked at a picture of a close friend, reported neurobiologists Andreas Bartels and Semir Zeki of University College London.

The scans showed that the experience of romantic attraction activated the pockets of the brain containing a high concentration of receptors for dopamine, the chemical messenger that's closely tied to states of euphoria, craving, and addiction. Elevated levels of dopamine in the brain result in extremely focused attention and goal-directed behaviors. Dopamine also produces that soaring feeling, sleeplessness, trembling, and a pounding heart; in the worst-case scenario, it triggers mania, anxiety, addictive behaviors, and fear. *That's all MFDA.* No wonder Robert Palmer had a hit with his song "Addicted to Love" . . . he wasn't kidding.

Dopamine might also be the reason why you can become "addicted" to a guy and actually crave him. When your feelings are reciprocated, this can be extremely pleasurable, but when they're not, it can result in severe MFDA.

Norepinephrine, a chemical derivative of dopamine, can heighten attention span and increase short-term memory, hyperactivity, sleeplessness, and goal-oriented behavior. This is why you're able to recall the smallest details of your beloved, including a mental transcript of everything that was said on a date. (And later you can obsess on it!)

When lovers are first captivated, Fisher contends, they often show signs of elevated dopamine levels: increased energy, less need for sleep or food, focused attention, and exquisite delight in the smallest details of their new love. However, people in long-term, committed relationships often lament that the initial surge, the euphoric sensation—meaning their dopamine production is in high gear—isn't there all the time, as it was in those early days.

The Four Manifestations of MFDA: Mental, Emotional, Behavioral, and Physical

Dating anxiety affects how you think, feel, and act. From the racing thoughts that keep you up at night to the butterflies in your stomach, the symptoms can be painful *and* exhilarating.

Julie played all of her conversations with Sam over and over again in her mind. Her anxious thoughts triggered uneasy feelings that led to disruptive behaviors such as the constant calling, texting, and the potentially embarrassing "run-in" with Sam at the hamburger joint. When he didn't return her messages and she couldn't find him at lunch, this revved up her MFDA, and she began to feel *anxious physical symptoms:* jitteriness and eventually sleeplessness.

Like many women, Julie was exhausted and emotionally over-wrought. She wasn't making great decisions, especially when she allowed Sam to come over for the 2 A.M. booty call. This derailed the potential consummation of all Four Pillars of Intimacy!

Let's look more closely at the four manifestations of MFDA in action. You'll begin to recognize how disruptive each of these can be to your dating experience.

Mental Symptoms of MFDA

Anxiety gets in the way of your dating life and can cost you a great love if it goes undiagnosed and untreated. The danger is the manner in which it distorts the reality of your experiences, causing you to misinterpret signs and signals that are crucial to a relationship's success or its potential to hit the skids.

Anxious thinking comes in myriad forms and is often referred to as *automatic negative thoughts* (ANTs). Maybe you've heard the expression "stinking thinking," made famous by 12-step programs like Alcoholics Anonymous. This mind-set is limiting and works against you in your dating life because ANTs are irrational thoughts that have little or no basis in reality. However, due to their spontaneous nature, you have to be highly cognizant of their presence and avoid acting on them in order to actually change your experiences.

It's really helpful to look at the mental *construct* of your dating environment. If MFDA is present, you'll make decisions that don't reflect your true intentions because anxiety distorts your view. ANTs are extremely destructive because they impose artifice on the reality of a situation, leading to damaging behaviors that ultimately dictate the direction of your love life. They cause you to act in disempowered and defensive ways designed to protect you from getting emotionally hurt again.

If you haven't learned a way of thinking about dating that assists you in the attainment of the Four Pillars of Intimacy, then regardless of your age and experience, your mental process is going to be infested with negative thoughts. It's inevitable. But as you read the following chapters and become more familiar with our concepts, you'll rid yourself of these defensive mental strategies and become more open when it comes to new dating opportunities.

What are the patterns of limiting thoughts that you need to banish from your life? Let's examine some of the mental manifestations of MFDA.

Recurring Thoughts. When it comes to MFDA, one of the most common symptoms is having recurring thoughts, which run through your head on a nonstop loop. Their purpose is to ease your fear by trying to control the unknown. It's a kind of self-talk done to make you feel better and less anxious when faced with dating uncertainty.

These thoughts often occur in patterns. Let's say you're wondering about a guy you're dating, so you keep playing the same five-minute phone conversation with him over and over again in your mind, trying to gain clarity through repetition. It's just like when Julie was hanging on Sam's every word and then repeating them to herself to make her MFDA seem less intense. She was

constantly thinking about what he said, what she said, and who said what first.

Another aspect of these recurring thoughts is when you find yourself asking again and again, *Why didn't he call? What could I have done differently so he would have called me? Was I too sexually forward? Does he think I'm easy?* It's by talking to yourself through these thoughts that you're attempting to relieve anxiety and calm your worries about *him.*

Recurring thoughts can limit romantic potential. Over and over again, year after year, guy after guy, your mind is a storehouse of thoughts and observations that you go to when you need guidance. You may sometimes think, *I'm too busy with work. It's not the right time for me. I don't have time to wait around because my clock is ticking. And if he's not perfect, forget it. Anyway, this guy was rude to a waiter so he's probably a mean person.* . . . These thoughts thwart your chances for romance by cutting off new dating experiences.

Repetitive Images. These are similar to repetitive thoughts but with a twist. (But not like the *Cosmo* trick Julie used!) Repetitive *images* are like a streaming video in your mind that plays in 3-D. When Julie was sitting home eating her Lean Cuisine lasagna, she was playing back the home movie (in her mind) about her great date with Sam.

Have *you* ever caught yourself mentally hitting the pause button so you could replay the "good parts," such as the first kiss or the time you tumbled into bed with what's-his-name? (Well, um, sorry that he's gone already.)

These repetitive images occur from the MFDA you're experiencing. It's your mind trying to get rid of your fear and control the unknown. The defense mechanism of repetitive images works to try to soothe the uncertainties in your dating life by creating an *illusion of knowledge* about what you *think* is going on. Your mind carefully edits and selects the vital data that you believe supports the evidence you're trying to gather.

For example, you want to know if he likes you, so you push the mental play button to try to recall how he feels about you, but what you're really doing is watching your own edited version of events. You dissect how he greeted you and whether he hugged or kissed you. You unconsciously craft your own "home movies," so when you push the mental play button to "learn" about your love life, you're really just watching your distorted perception of what happened.

We know that Julie "saw" Sam kissing her on the boat with Barry White crooning sexy tunes in the background. That's pure romance—so where did it go wrong?

Oh, yeah, she left out the part where she overheard him making plans with his ex for a weekend in Vegas for "business." She also didn't want to believe it when he said that it wasn't a good time to meet his family yet or when he introduced her to his friends as his *friend*—not his *girlfriend*. Instead, she played the image in her head that featured the two of them in that damn Jacuzzi in "their" future winter home. The movie she created in her mind came complete with passionate R-rated kisses (or better yet, X-rated)!

When Sam wasn't calling her, she also began to picture those lips kissing another woman and allowed that image to briefly tear her up inside. So she decided to return to the first image, make it even better than it actually was, and hit the play button again, looking for some mental soothing for her MFDA.

Another aspect of these recurring images is playing a certain scene from your last date or romanticizing the various encounters over and over again in your mind to figure out "what went wrong." Julie remembered saying good-bye to Sam after that sexy escapade on the boat. They were at her front door and she impulsively hugged him.

By endlessly playing back specific scenes, she ultimately drowned herself in questions: *Was that the wrong thing to do? Did he think I was too forward with that hug?* In her quest to find answers—any answers—she used these recurring pictures to alleviate her MFDA symptoms.

Idealization. This mental manifestation of MFDA occurs when you meet a guy who seems to embody all of your hopes and dreams. It's dangerous to fall for the *idealized* image (rather than the actual individual) just because it seems to fit your vision of your soul mate. Everyone envisions what their ideal mate is like. Which characteristics or qualities make up *your* perfect man? Is your *him* a doctor, lawyer, or rock musician who looks like Bono?

In Julie's mind, her ideal man had to be tall, dark, handsome, and look great in a suit. She thought her George Clooney (*him*) was the perfect combo of sexy and smart, so she blindly embraced Sam and dismissed all other guys who didn't fit that type. She unknowingly limited her dating potential by focusing on one man because he became her idealization.

Putting a guy (or certain traits) on a pedestal without a means to honestly evaluate his potential is what causes many women to fall victim to idealization. MFDA makes you believe that your perfect match only comes around once in a lifetime, so when you meet a man who *somewhat fits* the bill, you worry that you won't find his type or anything else that good again. He's your ideal, so he's become the greatest guy in the entire world in your mind (because of this manifestation of MFDA). Come on! Suddenly this stranger becomes your idealization of *everything* despite the fact that he's about to lose his job and there are rumors of a drinking problem. You can't even think an ill thought about him or your own personal Prince Charming will certainly slip through the cracks. You think, *He's the One! I may never find a guy this great again, so I've got to make this work at all costs. If this is my only shot, I'll give it my all to land my dream man.*

In college, Julie met a guy named Josh who played guitar and insisted his band was going to the top. She was really into musicians in those days (stemming from a Guns N' Roses fixation left over from high school) and told her friends, "I knew right away that Josh was the One because he's so different and special. He's not what you think. . . ."

Say *what?* Her MFDA caused her to enter a committed relationship with Josh within a couple weeks of meeting him, and she didn't know that he didn't think he'd be ready to settle down until he was collecting Social Security. To make matters worse, he repeatedly told her that she was a *keeper,* but he didn't hide the fact that he was dating other women. He loved it when his "groupies" would throw themselves at him.

Julie would have preferred being exclusive with him, but she was willing to take whatever she could get for a while because she thought that he'd be hers in the end. Like many women we've met, she was willing to *wait it out.* She continued to accommodate Josh, telling her gal pals, "He's so amazing. And I just feel like all these other women want him for the same reasons I do, so I just can't walk away."

In talking with us, many women like Julie (and maybe even you) have learned to see that this mental symptom of MFDA caused them to put themselves in situations (and maintain them) that were on the complete opposite spectrum of what they or you would ever want (or truly be able to withstand) because idealization convinced them that they'd found what they were looking for in a partner.

All-or-Nothing Thinking. This form of MFDA is also used to soothe your mind, and it has to do with seeing things as black or white and right or wrong. Here's how it works: Either you see *him* as perfect, or if the dating situation doesn't match your ideal image, you see it as a total failure and blow it off.

You may pick out a flaw, exaggerate its importance, and think, *He's not good enough. I'm out.*

Remember the episode of *Sex and the City* when Charlotte said that she'd immediately dump a guy if he brought her carnations because they're just "filler flowers"? Carrie's boyfriend responded, "Wow, you would dump a guy for bringing you flowers?" Charlotte looked at him like he was crazy and asserted that a man who'd bring such cheap flowers would certainly be cheap in all other ways.

All-or-nothing thinking has become recognizable evidence of a major dating problem. Anxiety on this scale involves drastic

choices and quickly making up your mind based on limited information. It's a way to defend against possible hurt feelings in a dating situation. You're protecting yourself from the uncertainty of dating, and MFDA makes you do crazy things to alleviate your fear of the unknown.

Charlotte would have shut a guy down without understanding his intentions or knowing anything about him. It was easier for her to decide that he's "all bad" (or in this case, cheap in all other ways). I (Dr. C) say that women use this defense mechanism to *qualify* men completely in *one way*—rather than taking the emotional risk of getting to know a guy really well and gathering a lot of information about whether or not he's generous. (And maybe carnations are his favorite flower—who knows at this point?)

Another aspect of this all-or-nothing mind-set is when it causes you to make rash decisions, such as "I *know* he's the One," or at the other extreme, "I'm not going to find anyone I really like, so I'm just going to give up on dating." You're cutting out so many possibilities that could exist for you. (If only you had a dating method that you could rely on . . . oh, wait, you do now!) This symptom can manifest after a first date even though you don't really know the guy you went out with. Yet based on limited information, *you* decide that you want to make him your boyfriend and blindly jump into a serious relationship.

A few years ago when she was just starting out in Chicago, Julie ran into Keith at her high-school reunion. They went home together that night because the old feelings they had for each other in the past were stirred up once more. But she couldn't resist the urge to label Keith the moment she met up with him.

Keith worked at a printing shop and seemed content with his blue-collar status. However, Julie had higher standards as an ad exec and had no real intentions of dating him . . . but she'd been without a boyfriend for a while and was lonely, a little horny, and plenty drunk—not an ideal situation to be making all-or-nothing choices. She decided that Keith wasn't "relationship material." Still, she went home with him that night to have sex "just for fun." They had a really good time, which ended that night.

Well, until a week passed, when Julie called Keith again. Huh? Yep. During that time, she'd made a "miraculous" discovery.

After using her all-or-nothing thinking to its fullest potential, she gathered some unexpected material. She *saw* that they really had a lot in common and realized that maybe she'd judged him prematurely. (By the way, she later discovered that he made more money than she did as a junior ad exec living on mac and cheese from the box—*oops*.)

Money wasn't the only issue here; she labeled Keith as "undatable" out of her own anxiety. She feared his rejection but masked it by convincing herself that there could never be anything there because he had a blue-collar job. It would have been much harder for her to think, *This is a guy I could like. Now I'm going to leave my high-school reunion, and he may or may not call me.* So rather than deal with the MFDA symptoms, she soothed her anxiety by making up her mind quickly and dismissing him.

This caused her even *more* anxiety because she then tried to date him seriously, but by being so casual with him and not showing any interest beyond a "good time," he only thought of her as a booty call and didn't want to date *her* seriously. (Men also use all-or-nothing thinking, and now he labeled her as "kinda slutty.") Her all-or-nothing mind-set bit her in the ass. *Again.*

Overgeneralization. Many of our clients come to us with complaints such as, "I always end up heartbroken" or "I never meet nice guys." This is a limiting way of thinking that serves the purpose of making things seem more certain—thus, making the dating environment less ambiguous. It's also a defensive dating practice. What happens with this mental manifestation of MFDA is that you experience a single negative event—such as a bad breakup or romantic rejection—and then make a blanket statement about how things *always* or *never* happen. Overgeneralization also works the other way. Remember how Julie felt when Sam called her out of the blue? She thought he was the most amazing guy because of this *one act* of calling kindness.

Nothing always or never happens unless you subconsciously support that belief. For instance, Julie wants to believe that dating is always hard and never fun, so she overgeneralizes to support her idea that maybe she should just avoid dating.

Our client Linda was a master overgeneralizer. After reentering the dating arena for the first time in years, she didn't meet anyone right away, and it caused her to state how awful the dating environment was now. Even after meeting a couple of nice guys, she kept affirming her belief that there were no good men in the entire universe.

You shouldn't think in terms of *never* or *always* because this is quite limiting! There are many things in life that are possible when you learn to allow the excitement of the unknown to enter each new day. When you can stop overgeneralizing, unexpected opportunities can enter your life in amazing ways.

Obsession. According to the breathy voice in that old Calvin Klein commercial, "Between love and madness lies Obsession." The idea of an obsession is something that the fashion industry made sexy, but for most people, this is very unsexy, as it's a manifestation of MFDA that can wreak havoc in your dating life.

So what is *obsession* besides a word that many think means "crazy"? In some ways, it does have to do with something that's "out of control," because it's when you can't stop thinking about a guy you just met and believe that you're going mad without him. Red alert: You're dwelling in your MFDA obsession zone.

I (Dr. C) say that obsessions are compulsive preoccupations with a fixed idea. They're often accompanied by symptoms of anxiety and aren't eliminated by surface-level reasoning. This usually happens when you meet and then fall in love with someone quickly. You're 100 percent convinced he's absolutely amazing and you can't stop thinking about how much you want him to be your boyfriend, so you immediately begin to invest your emotions into the potential. When he backs away, you only want him more! You're compulsively drawn to this guy because of your MFDA.

Have you ever called a guy you liked a few times a day? Did you call the moment you woke up before you even brushed your teeth? Have you cruised by his house although it's ten miles away and he could have spotted you through his living-room window? Have you talked about him with others as if he's your boyfriend? Have you dissected his every word, thought, and emotion with a pack of girlfriends?

This manifestation of mental MFDA causes severe distress because it's limiting by its very nature. Great relationships don't come from impatient, obsessive desires. (And by the way, he probably *did* see you cruise by his house, which is why he thinks you're too clingy and isn't calling.) Pay attention to any obsessive thoughts, because they can be destructive to your dating life if you're not careful.

Mind Reading. We've put this last because we think it's the most amusing of all the mental manifestations of MFDA. How could we possibly say that something like this is funny? Well, how often do women sit around and read the minds of the men who confuse them? It's a national pastime!

The good news is that this is a harmless symptom of MFDA as long as you recognize it for what it is. Mind reading causes you to jump to conclusions even though very little information has been assembled. The tendency to interpret things instantly despite the fact that there's no evidence to support your conclusion is another attempt to soothe the anxiety of uncertainty. If you don't know what's really taking place in the mind of a guy you're interested in dating, mind reading can temporarily make you feel better.

The certainty in which women read the minds of the men they date is astonishing. As an expert "mind reader," you *know* for sure that Steven isn't calling back because you're not a size six, and he's dating 12 other women who are far prettier and have bigger boobs—natural ones!

You're swimming in negativity although there's no real evidence that what you're thinking is even remotely accurate. When

mind reading, you're limiting the possibilities for a relationship because you don't really know the truth.

After many first dates, Julie would tell herself, *He didn't try to kiss me, so he doesn't find me attractive. There's no point in going on a second date.* That may be true, but by declaring it so quickly, based solely on her mind-reading skills, she may ultimately be causing something special to dissolve before it has a chance to form.

Emotional Symptoms of MFDA

Fear. Fear is a crippling aspect of emotional MFDA because it can affect your ability to form relationships. When fear is present, it causes you to date defensively. No one likes to feel fearful, so when this emotion enters your dating life, you'll immediately try to soothe the anxiety.

For example, you encounter a guy you like but fear that he won't meet your emotional needs, so you choose to bail out now before you get hurt. Maybe you're subconsciously afraid of meeting a great guy, and in response, you settle for someone who's less than what you desire. Or perhaps you go on a date with a terrific guy and because you fear that no one this cool will ever come along again, you jump the gun and destroy any potential. You might fear that you won't find the One before your biological clock stops ticking—or if you'll ever meet him at all. Fear could cause any number of reactions within you, and not one of them is likely to benefit a new relationship.

Fear causes you to act in ways that are contrary to developing a dynamic partnership, and it may even prevent you from reentering the dating environment altogether (especially after a breakup or divorce). It can also creep up later in the process when you start dating one person exclusively. You may be constantly afraid that the relationship could end suddenly even though everything is going great.

All of these fears can result in a particular aspect of MFDA that we call *fear-based dating.* Since dating is an activity that involves a significant amount of emotional risk, fear-based daters are reluctant to take any risks or engage in any new activities that may not work. They don't really put themselves out there and instead build up walls to protect themselves from getting hurt. The fearful dater imposes restraints because of mistrust. Within intimate relationships, the fear of being shamed or ridiculed causes their dating lives to be unfruitful.

The fear of criticism, disapproval, or rejection is so intense for some women that fear-based daters will go to great efforts to avoid (real or imagined) abandonment. These women are deeply afraid of being "hung out to dry" like they were in the past; thus, they avoid taking any chances.

When you're dating from a fearful place and aren't willing to get involved with people unless you're certain of it working out, this is MFDA at its most heinous, because it will destroy potential relationships.

Depression. Depression is a form of emotional MFDA and is probably the most familiar—feeling blue, down-and-out, bummed, hopeless, or sad (for extended periods of time). These are all recognizable signs of MFDA, and the agony of hopelessness about love causes serious depression in many women.

For example, are there are still songs that bring tears to your eyes (your song with him) and make you doubt that you'll ever experience love again? You can't enter a T.G.I. Friday's without feeling sad, because years ago you stopped there with John, who loved the spicy wings. (You can't even buy frozen wings from the supermarket without hauling out the Kleenex.) You can't ever go to Hawaii either (never again in your entire life) because that was your and his "dream place." You know that you'll never be happy anywhere.

If your depression persists (you can't wake up in the morning, you don't want to leave your house, or you feel suicidal), please seek a professional counselor or therapist. We'll also help

you deal with less serious forms of depression in the groundwork section of this book.

Euphoria. People usually associate this state of being with the highest form of interpersonal chemistry, love, and excitement. How could we categorize euphoria as a symptom of emotional MFDA?

Euphoria can be deceptive because your mood is inflated—actually elevated beyond your normal waking state—and it can leave you feeling high, like you're on a drug. You may be thinking, *Sounds pretty good if you ask me!*

Meeting someone you have relationship potential with is really exciting, but after you meet him, then what? How do you capture lightning in a bottle and turn that spark into the roaring fire of passion? You may meet someone new and experience instant chemistry, feeling as if the answer to your prayers is standing in front of you, and now it's safe to be swept off your feet. But you still must be cautious.

What you're feeling may be a number of things, including your need for a connection with someone, which leads you to drop all of your traditional defenses. Your euphoric state is overwhelming and causes you to inflate this man's worth and importance in your life at this early stage of the dating process. Doing so will make you act in extreme ways and further feed into your MFDA.

This manifestation of MFDA can also allow you to experience the high of a new guy to an excessive degree. If the feelings you have are out of proportion with the reality of your dating life, then you're in trouble. You have these crazy, intense feelings about him and he seems so perfect, although you've just been out for coffee with him one time.

Is it possible that it's love at first sight? Of course anything is possible, but the majority of relationships that are based on those quick flash feelings crash, burn, and leave you feeling empty.

The euphoric feeling can pump you up with so much excitement that you can't stop talking to your friends about him or stop planning your future down to the type of SUV you'll buy for your 2.4 future kids. You're distracted at work and don't really listen to your friends and their problems. At times, you're feeling on top of the world, but then you also feel strangely low at other moments. At night you try to sleep, but your thoughts are racing with anticipation of the next fix—as if you have an addiction to this emotional high. As the relationship fades in time, what are you left with?

This is the danger of emotional manifestations of MFDA.

Behavioral Symptoms of MFDA

Oh, fun—here's yet another aspect of dating anxiety! Once your mental and emotional manifestations of MFDA have had their way with you, you now begin to produce external, action-able, behavioral symptoms.

Would a successful, smart woman like Julie have done a "drive-by" if her mental and emotional anxieties had not gotten so out of control? Have you ever done the drive-by, or gone some-where or done something in order to relieve your dating anxiety? If so, your MFDA has gotten to you.

After Sam stopped calling Julie completely, she decided she'd escape her own MFDA by avoiding dating at all costs and staying home with a carton of ice cream! Her *inaction* was actually an *action* in *reaction* to MFDA. After a few weeks of this behavior and a five-pound weight gain, she changed her mind and let her friend Amanda take her to a hot downtown club.

Julie put on her cutest outfit (her MFDA tells her that men look for external beauty, so if she's going to catch a man, she'd better look hot!) and told Amanda that she was really excited to meet some new guys. Once at the club, she unknowingly acted cold and unapproachable toward each man who seemed interested in her.

Her standoffishness was a subconscious attempt to prevent her from future heartbreak—which is a behavioral response to anxiety—but it also prevented her from meeting anyone new.

Intimate Contact. Now it's time to talk about what happens between the sheets, because MFDA affects your sex life in many ways. When you're feeling anxious, often the most comfortable way to remove anxiety is to get as close to the object of your desire as possible—going beyond words to the realm of physical contact.

This desire for closeness can be achieved by holding hands, kissing, or having sexual intercourse, which is a deeply personal act that tends to bond people closer together. For some, it can be a wonderful opportunity to release tension once in a while, but we must caution you: *Casual sex and relationship-focused dating don't mix.*

Julie felt that as a modern woman, she was comfortable with casual sex every now and then, but later recognized that this seldom resulted in the types of connections she was ultimately looking for in life. However, her MFDA pressured her to find a guy and quickly bond with him. She'd sleep with him right away for fear of losing him to another woman (more behavioral manifestations of MFDA surfacing).

Despite her three-date rule, Julie occasionally slept with a guy on the second date to prevent him, she thought, from being interested in other women. She believed this was harmless because sex has been liberated in our society, and there's no need to withhold it from a guy to make him like you.

Our proven dating technique, the **Stop Wondering Method**—from here on out called the SW Method—doesn't come down to something as simple as not having sex with a guy . . . at least, not entirely. (More on that later when we get to the second date and beyond.) In the SW Method, *sex is the consummation of a committed relationship.*

For a guy, sexual contact with an anxious female makes him question the value of the potential relationship. I (Ryan) want to explain this in more detail. When sex comes almost immediately, a guy thinks that this girl must be easy and probably sleeps with different men frequently. Let me clue you in on a secret about guys now: Men think that hard work results in victory. If something comes too easily, we don't value it.

Of course, many men will have sex with a willing woman (or women) without even the slimmest intent of pursuing a relationship with her. For many of the women we've consulted with over the years, we've noticed a commonality: She thinks the sex will bond them; he thinks she's not worth it because she's easy if she gives it up too soon.

For women, this "I want you to choose me" sex represents the anxiety associated with the desire to consummate a relationship quickly so that the man will commit. However, having sex too early often means that the opposite will be true.

Julie told her friend Abby, "I slept with Sam because I was worried that if he didn't see how great our connection was within a few dates, he'd start looking for other girls."

Surrendering to these anxious thoughts and feelings results in rash behavior. And this mind-set, which is a result of an uncertain and confusing dating experience, causes sex to become a desperate attempt to maintain closeness—either to keep him from moving on to the next girl or to get him naked and near you because it makes you feel safe and loved.

You want him to immediately like you while also fearing he'll lose interest. This anxiety is tied to feeling insecure, thinking that you might not have qualities he will like, which is, of course, deeply rooted in your subconscious MFDA.

Physical contact is a special gift and bond; within the SW Method, you'll learn how to cultivate this special connection in a way that's reminiscent of your adolescent first loves, where there was simplicity, sweetness, raw passion, openness, and the pulse-pounding thrill of discovery.

Technological Contact. When you call, text-message, or e-mail a guy to ease your uncertainties and dating anxieties, you've entered another realm of your MFDA behavioral symptoms. Have you ever wanted to know once and for all if you're *exclusive* with someone? Have you ever called a guy immediately after leaving a voice mail to see if he'd pick up?

After Julie was single for a while, her MFDA began to haunt her again. Out of anxiety and loneliness, she decided to Google an old college boyfriend who she knew had a rocky marriage. She wanted to check the pulse on his status. She knew this was sort of crazy, but she couldn't control the impulse because her feelings of loneliness caused her to act out and finally call him. When his wife answered and Julie hung up on her, she knew she was out of control.

You were given the technology to date in new ways, and cell phones even give you a signal in the wilds of Alaska. When your educational system failed to teach Dating 101, it also forgot to instruct you on how to use technology in dating. It's a key dating skill now because you have constant and instant access to men, but anxiety can cause you to abuse this freedom or techno privilege. We'll teach you how to use technology in later chapters so that it's a *tool* for you during this process, rather than a dating liability.

Physical Symptoms of MFDA

The mere idea of dating can produce anxious physiological responses in your skin (sweating), muscles (tightness), lungs (rapid breaths), and heart (pounding). These are commonly referred to as somatic symptoms. You experience these heightened arousal states and increased stress levels in your physical body as threshold indicators of excitement.

MFDA produces a range of real physical symptoms, which can be pleasurable as well as distressing. These include "butterflies," being "on edge," or feeling a bit "ramped up" with nervous energy about an impending date. You can't seem to calm yourself down when consumed by a new guy you're dating.

Another physical symptom of MFDA is sweaty palms, which is normal because the body has millions of sweat glands, and more than half are found in the hands. But when the body becomes agitated—through extreme temperatures or extreme dating anxiety (one and the same . . . who knew?)—those glands release sweat to help cool the body back down to its optimal temperature. Sweating is a physical symptom of being nervous on a date, so you have to learn how to cool yourself down and dissolve the MFDA in order to stop the excessive perspiration. (Gross, right?)

Maybe you felt your own racing heart when a cute guy entered the room, walked right up to you, kissed you, and . . . well, *if* that happened, your heart would have probably beat out of your chest. These symptoms often signal the beginning of the sexual-response cycle, and, of course, it's pleasurable because your body is getting aroused, anticipating that these desires will be satisfied. In this case, your racing heart is an exhilarating experience.

How about those times when you felt your heart practically beat out of your chest from being overcome by a sense of dread or fear? When the dating environment threatens you, your heart will race in a dating panic attack. This form of MFDA is related to loneliness, anticipation of something great around the corner, a desperate need for confirmation of feelings, or euphoric states.

Have you ever had someone take your breath away, cause you to gasp, or even to hyperventilate? This may sound extreme, but MFDA can actually affect your breathing in much the same way as a racing heart. Your breathing can become shallow when excited or agitated, because you're actually depriving your body of oxygen when it's in a stressed state as a result of MFDA.

Now What?

We've spent this chapter talking about all the manifestations of MFDA, and you might be feeling a little bummed out now. Yes, we know you're suffering, but the good news is that you just need to turn the page because a new class is about to be called into session. In the next chapters, we'll teach you how to beat MFDA, with a dating system that really works and will change your life forever.

Get ready. Let's go!

Chapter 2

The Dating Class You <u>Wish</u> You Had—
Session One

You were taught many lessons in school: how to write the letters of the alphabet, work complicated math problems, locate the Nile on a map, and even how to pass notes to your girlfriends in the back of the class. But of all the things you learned in school, chances are that you were never taught one of the most essential skills that profoundly influences the quality of your life: how to date in connection with the Four Pillars of Intimacy.

Even without fully realizing how dating ties in to the Four Pillars, you intuitively know that it can lead you to your life mate, which may be one of your most important endeavors. Finding the right partner can lead to a happy love life, amazing sex, and a dynamic relationship. That's what we all want, right?

You might have been taught how to get behind the wheel of a car and put the key in the ignition but not how to steer yourself successfully in a new romance. In the majority of relationships, most women have been driving out of control without so much as a learner's

permit. They close their eyes and put their stiletto to the metal, thinking the entire time that they'll reach their destination (a loving, committed relationship) by traveling as fast as possible along the way. I (Ryan) want to point out that the speed in which the modern world moves is deceptive, and when it comes to finding lasting love, it takes more skill than most people think to traverse all the obstacles and safely stay on course.

Think about this for a second: If you've never had any formal education in a specific subject—in this case, rather than driver's ed, we're referring to *dating ed*—then how can you expect to be an expert in that field? Without establishing a dating method for yourself, how can you create the ideal relationship that you want? No one you know has ever enrolled in a Dating 101 class, because it simply doesn't exist!

We're willing to bet that when it comes to dating, you've taught yourself almost everything you know—through blind luck, trial and error, and the notes that you and your girlfriends passed in class while your high-school teachers droned on about stuff you knew wouldn't be relevant in the real world.

However, the problem with not having any formal training is that you may not *really* know how to date, and this is one of the leading causes of MFDA. It doesn't matter what your age is, or your level of experience, because if you're still dating without clearly understanding the process, you're bound to be confused and frustrated in your encounters with men. Being smart and successful doesn't mean that you'll automatically know how to date effectively or form successful relationships.

Julie's long-held belief was that when she finally met Mr. Right, everything would just instantly fall into place. She believed that true love meant that a connection would be obvious to both of them and the whole dating process could be skipped. Each time she met a guy she thought was perfect—or even good enough—she expected the pieces to fit instantly and easily, without any confusing or awkward dating moments. Unfortunately, Julie has rarely found what she's looking for and has suffered a lot of heartache and disappointment along the way because the One hasn't magically shown up. She anxiously waits for her Prince Charming to appear, as she kisses one frog after another.

If dating is so important, then why doesn't anyone teach you how to do it properly? That's where we come in! So wipe your mental slate clean when it comes to your perception of the dating process, and let's start at the beginning. . . .

Everyone Has Their Own Definition of Dating

What does the word *dating* mean to *you?* Does it entail hanging out with a guy you like for a while before finding someone else who might have more spousal potential? Or is dating looking for someone you want to explore a relationship with to the exclusion of all others? Perhaps it involves waiting until one guy magically shows up on his white horse and you decide he's the One.

Does dating involve sex? If so, are you supposed to have sex with one person at a time, or should you hook up with new people on a regular basis? If you're dating someone, does it mean that he's your *boyfriend,* or are you *seeing* each other?

Just as we do with our clients, we'll begin by exploring your *personal* definition to help you better understand your perception of the dating process. Then we'll investigate more commonly held assumptions and ultimately define dating according to the SW Method.

How Do You Define Dating?

Take a moment to think about your personal definition of dating. Review the questions we listed in the previous paragraphs to guide you if nothing comes to mind right away.

Before we go any further, we also want to state this clearly: Whenever we have a quiz or exercise, remember that there are no right or wrong answers. There's no high or low score and no F's in this class, so be honest. No one is judging you (except maybe yourself), so let the truth fly. This will be liberating, and the information will be used later in this chapter and throughout the book as a reference point. If you can honestly assess your beliefs, it will help you tremendously, and you'll be able to successfully incorporate the SW Method into your life.

So please take a moment now to complete your class work. You may even want to write some thoughts down in the notes section at the end of the book. Remember, you're in dating class and there will be some fun, illuminating assignments that require a little reflection on your part. A few minutes should be enough time for this first lesson, but take more or less time as needed.

Come on—wasn't that fun!

Why Is Dating So Rough These Days? The Demise of Courtship

Between the 1920s and the 1960s, dating was a social pastime for most teenagers. The ritual of dating was very specific and purposeful, and there were traditional, clear-cut roles: A woman's ultimate goal was to find a husband, get married, and have children.

To get the ring or her "Mrs. Degree," a woman had to engage in a formal process known as courtship. The young man was referred to as a gentleman caller because he had to follow a strict protocol when "calling" on a woman. In order to take a young woman on a date (and return her home at a designated time), her father's permission had to be granted. If the date went well, they liked each other, and their parents agreed that it was a good match, they'd become a couple who were then dubbed "going steady." This meant that they were going *slow and steady* while exploring their romantic potential through a series of formal dates on the way to marriage. Physical intimacy happened gradually and slowly.

My, how things have changed!

Of course, there are still people who practice traditional courtship—especially when reinforced by their particular religious or ethnic group; however, the modern dating environment has made this more challenging.

The women's movement and the sexual revolution both conspired to shape (and forever change) the modern dating culture. With the sexual revolution in the 1960s and early '70s, the concept of "free love" allowed open sexual expression to become a voice of personal liberation.

Birth control pills, first introduced in 1960, enabled women to have sex without the fear of pregnancy. The freeing idea that you didn't have to get married to have sex may seem old-fashioned and even prudish these days, but when this first occurred, it was truly revolutionary. Sex was indeed a place where men and women could be equal; now they could both enjoy it freely. Yet while we were very concerned about men and women enjoying sex, most people didn't realize that they enjoy it differently.

Like It or Not, Women and Men *Are* Different When It Comes to Sex

I (Dr. C) want to explain this further.

The hormone oxytocin is a neurotransmitter in the brain that helps us form bonds with others. Research has shown that the higher the level of oxytocin, the more empathetic and less aggressive an individual will be. This hormone also links the verbal centers in the brain and stimulates a nurturing response within people. Higher levels of oxytocin in mothers enable them to form

deep bonds and respond to the emotional needs of their spouse, children, and friends.

Oxytocin is naturally released in response to a variety of environmental stimuli, including nipple stimulation in lactating women, uterine or cervical stimulation during sex, or as the result of a baby moving down the birth canal. During sex, the increase in oxytocin causes a woman to intensely bond with her partner, creating romantic attachment. Just about the only time a man experiences a surge of this hormone is during orgasm, which allows him to bond with his partner as well. However, after orgasm a man's oxytocin level returns to its normal state, while a woman's level remains consistently higher. This is why a man may be compelled to say "I love you" during sex but may not feel like saying it much afterward when the woman is longing to hear reassuring words of affection. This is also why sleeping together too soon may be more dangerous for a woman than a man.

While the benefits of this newfound age of sexual liberation are plentiful, there was a downside that slipped between the cracks. The tie between emotional and sexual intimacy was blurred and then practically severed, which has resulted in a great deal of chaos and confusion for many women.

Some women still try to adhere to the courtship process, as their families continue to uphold this ritual, yet the overall dating environment (where young women have become famous for making sex tapes) makes it difficult to practice. By removing all aspects of the traditional guidelines, we modern-age daters have *all* lost the wonderful simplicity that comes with those set rules and formality. We've also lost the clear process where one person (usually the male) contacts another person (usually the female) to arrange a date. After that first date, and if all goes well, a process of *dating* ensues.

Today there usually isn't a formalized dating process. While we're not advocating a strict, old-school practice per se, we do want to borrow certain characteristics from the courtship *ritual* as we redefine dating for the 21st-century female.

We know it sounds rather simplistic, but formality is something many women are craving again. Casual dating may be fun at first, but it eventually becomes unfulfilling and often leads to pain, frustration, and loneliness. You wouldn't be reading this book right now if you were happy with today's dating scene. We've been hearing again and again that women are dreaming of having relationships that are more than just hanging out and hooking up, which usually doesn't lead anywhere. In fact, some women have even told us that they haven't been on a formal date—or a "real date"—in years, yet they've "hung out" with various men for sometimes months at a time.

The reason why Julie thought Sam was the One was because their date at that little Italian restaurant was her first formal date in five years, and she figured that it must have really meant something. When was the last time someone asked you out on a formal date, or even a second or third real date?

When Julie was a graduate student, she saw an aspiring actor named Russell for three months but never went on a formal date with him. She explains, "We met at a dinner party for my friend's birthday and drank wine all night and told each other jokes. He practically moved in the next day.

"He was an aspiring actor who had lots of free time, and since I was in school and studying, I was usually home during the day. I really liked him. It was so fun and easy between us—it got to the point where he'd come over practically unannounced after the first week, and it was comfortable," she recalls.

"Comfortable"? Is that also what you want in your life?

Julie remembers that she didn't mind "hangin'" with Russ but always wondered if they were exclusive. She wasn't even sure if they were really dating! One minute he'd kiss her and in the next he'd point out "hot chicks" on the street. He obviously thought they had an understanding, which she failed to grasp. Julie was participating in a phenomenon we call the *death of the date* and the birth of the hook-up culture.

The Hang-Out, Hook-Up Culture

In the absence of formal dating and a classic "getting to know you" process, you've probably had very few planned dates or ones you could anticipate for days in advance. When we've asked women to define dating, nine out of ten times they've said that "it's hanging out and hooking up with someone you like while determining if something more is possible." This is a casual approach that relies on a certain "whatever feels good in the moment" dating philosophy.

The term *hooking-up* is a Gen Y contribution to the modern dating landscape; and those born after 1977 know that this signifies sexual encounters that are brief, sometimes fun, and usually not the first step toward a meaningful relationship. Hooking-up typically involves anything physical within the range of kissing, intercourse, and oral sex. It's either with a stranger (the one-night-stand variety), a friend (with "benefits"), an acquaintance (tastefully referred to as an "F-buddy"), or with a guy you may actually want as a boyfriend. Hooking-up in this last case seems positively goal directed, but as you'll see in the SW Method, this form of casual sex can be misleading and often leads to heartbreak.

What we say next probably seems obvious by now, but we'll state it here for the record: *Hanging out and hooking-up are counterproductive to developing emotional intimacy. Successful dating requires taking thoughtful and formal steps rather than casual missteps.*

Anyone who's been in a "hang out and hook up" situation knows that it's commonplace to *never know* where you stand, and it's nearly impossible to make the jump into a serious relationship. This is just a land mine of confusion, so please be careful where you step because you might blow up your heart.

Before meeting Sam, Julie's last date had been with a banker named Ted. After they met, she spent the next three weeks "hanging out" with him at his place or hers. At the time, this arrangement felt comfortable to her because she didn't want to be that girl who puts pressure on a guy by demanding fancy dates at expensive places. They had so much in common, so it seemed safe to keep things casual, order some pizza, watch movies, and make out.

"We have similar backgrounds and ideals for the future. We were matched up in so many ways—it was almost like a dream," Julie recalled. After their initial formal blind date, they skipped the rest altogether and within the first week, they were hanging out practically every night in front of "Must See TV."

Julie reported, "He'd come over to my place and we'd watch a movie or something—although we rarely got to the movie. We had so much passion and chemistry; it was great. We'd have wine and take-out while getting cozy on the couch. It was a few blissful months until he got promoted at his company and had to start traveling more."

She was upset about all of his traveling, but she didn't really know him well enough to complain. They never talked about how he was going to be leaving town every month if he got the promotion and would never be available for a traditional relationship. Ted eventually explained to Julie that he really enjoyed hanging out with her, but he wasn't thinking about the future. He forgot to tell her that he had no intention of having a serious relationship because he was solely focused on his work. Over slices of pizza or while their clothes were coming off, he failed to mention that everything (including her) took a backseat to his ambition. Julie complained to her girlfriends that eventually the only time she saw Ted was late at night over at his house. "It was fine because I wanted to see him, but it also left me feeling like he cared a lot more about his job than me."

We asked her when things started to feel like they were off track. She replied, "Even though the chemistry was amazing, I guess things felt off the whole time because I never really knew where I stood with him. I haven't spoken to Ted in two weeks, and I want so badly to believe that it was more than just sex for him because I really liked him. I just can't understand why he'd choose his job over me. Maybe I blew it, but I don't know."

It wasn't Julie's fault that this happened, and Ted isn't necessarily a jerk. Julie never knew where she stood because if you

just hang out and hook up with a guy, you'll never really know what's happening—and most likely, *nothing* is happening. By just hanging out, there isn't an established communication pattern between the two of you. There are no boundaries or structures set in place to assist your budding relationship. You're actually creating emotional involvement without a stable foundation to build on and guide your feelings.

The grand illusion of this dating environment is that you're spending more time together (in a casual way) and now act as comfortable as an old married couple. Although you're still in the initial dating stages, this implies that you're getting to know each other better—right? That's absolutely wrong. The truth is getting to know one another intimately actually takes time and involves interacting in real-life situations. Trust us, the guy who's just sitting on your couch all night, every night—and who isn't taking you out on dates—isn't letting you know who he *really* is. You need to see him out in the world, socializing at a work function, hanging out with his family, or even interacting with strangers on the street in order to learn about the real him.

The myth is that hook-up sex makes men and women closer emotionally. You may have been sexually intimate, but the truth is that you still may not know very much about him, what he wants in life, if he's seeing anyone else, or if he even wants a real relationship. This could leave you suffering from the agony and ecstasy of MFDA if you get caught in casual dating.

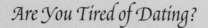

Are You Tired of Dating?

Although you may have engaged in years of fun and partying with friends and have met a few great guys along the way, perhaps you've grown tired of the dating scene. We get that you don't like bars and clubs anymore, and even if you do, you know it can be difficult to meet some-one who appears to have true potential. Maybe you feel that even with all the online-dating sites, it's still tough to find anybody to date—or take—seriously. Think about the following:

- Are you sick of dating but also worried and feeling pressure that you need to "settle down" soon and begin your "real" life?

- Do you hate dating but wonder how you'll ever meet *him* if you don't date anymore?

- Are you tired of enduring horrible first dates and feeling sad watching your friends marry and have children?

- Are you sick of having to RSVP to parties without the "+1" that they always include on your invitation?

How do you go from single to having a lasting relationship? It's not *dating* that's getting you. You're just not *approaching* dating in the right way.

Chapter 3

The Dating Environment—
How Times Have Changed!

We keep using the word *approach*, but what do we mean, exactly? By definition, an "approach" is a method used to accomplish a goal or solve a problem. In this case, the goal is love and the problem is finding the right guy to develop an intimate relationship with in this casual dating environment. There are many steps involved in getting from the first meeting to a committed relationship. Our founding principle is this: *Don't let him date you casually. Make him date you formally.*

Look at Julie, who thought that she shouldn't be too demanding with Sam because it would scare him away—that was her dating approach, and it didn't work. But Julie isn't alone in that manner of thinking. Our client Mary Beth used the same strategy. She told us, "I don't want to put pressure on guys. If they want me, they should make the effort, but I make it as easy and comfortable as possible. No pressure."

How did so many intelligent women pick up the same useless dating philosophy? Class is back in session!

 Wondering . . .

What You've Already Learned about Dating

Everyone has a unique dating approach that they've created in the absence of formal learning, and this has been repeatedly practiced over the years on every date you've ever had—whether you went out with a guy last night, last week, or last year. Although your dating know-how may change a bit over the years with new insights and experiences, the reality is that your first lessons, or initial imprints, are subconsciously lodged in your psyche.

Julie rattled off some of what she'd learned from her older sister: "Love is hard to find, so when you find the right guy, hold on tight or some other girl will steal him away." Even without a formal class, Julie was taught how to date from a trusted source who probably had her own MFDA. The information that Julie absorbed in her youth obviously didn't really help her out in the long run.

The reality is that most women we work with approach dating using what's commonly referred to as their "game plan." We don't think that dating is a game at all. And although no one likes to play games (at least not most people), playing *the game* is common among modern daters. What are some of the common dating approaches that women use? As you read, ask yourself if any of the following seem familiar to you. Did they help or hurt your chances of finding true love? Let's take a closer look.

Playing the Game

This dating approach includes everything having to do with "rules," "playing hard to get," or knowing someone who's viewed as a "player," an unattractive '90s term that implies multiple sexual liaisons with a variety of women. Let's try to get a better understanding of why games have become such a significant part of dating. It's obvious that people equate romantic pursuits with them when you look at common phrases such as "winning over the guy," "competing with other women" for a man, or "being up to the challenge" of finding the One. For many women, dating has been a lifelong challenge, requiring strategy, winning and losing, and "playing the field."

Playing the game or remaining detached, disinterested, cool, and aloof is a strategy that many women use to make themselves seem even more appealing to men. The object of the game is to "get" the guy, of course. The idea is to *win* at dating and influence your opponent's (the guy you're interested in) next move based on how you've played your cards. For example, a woman who's playing the game hopes that she can make herself seem more attractive to a guy by playing hard to get, which will (hopefully) cause him to take the initiative.

It would appear that waiting days on end to call someone back or pretending not to be interested—when in fact, you are—would work. It even seems to be a good strategy for protecting yourself from MFDA because you don't let your emotions come into play too quickly and you keep a safe distance—sounds perfect! The immediate advantage of using this method is that it can make you feel like you're in control of the situation, which is actually an impulsive reaction to your MFDA. Playing games with someone may also temporarily alleviate your anxiety because by being dishonest about your true thoughts and feelings, you can avoid feeling vulnerable. You can stay within your comfort zone as he pursues you, while you decide whether or not he can "win your heart." But does it really work?

A woman who uses this strategy is often less focused on getting to know an individual and more focused on *winning him over*, which means that even when she gets the guy, he may not be who she thought he was. Let me (Ryan) shed some light on this: Guys are often slow to involve their emotions in new relationships. So if there's game playing involved, many men will be turned off by the dishonest and deceptive aspects of this approach. No one likes to be lied to or *played with*. It's no wonder why so many people who have online-dating profiles specify that they want someone who is "honest and doesn't play games!"

"I'll Know It When I See It"

This approach involves *not* dating and believing that when you've met the man of your dreams, you'll *just know it* and dating won't be necessary. The assumption here is that the moment your eyes meet across a crowded room, you'll both know that it's true love. This may seem very familiar from the numerous love stories (featured in the romantic movies you've seen or stories in the media) that are built around the idea of love at first sight. Many women believe that in an unexpected moment in the future, when the timing is perfect and the stars align, something magical will happen. They'll undoubtedly know love when they "see" it.

There are some couples who claim that their love originated from the intensity of the moment they first met. All things are possible in life, and we know that this is one of the ways in which love blooms. However, patiently waiting until the moment when your soul mate just falls into your lap isn't a good approach to dating. Even if you're sure that you'll know it when you see it, it still doesn't mean that you don't have to date and get to know a guy on a deeper level. An instant does not a relationship make!

The truth is that the "I'll know it when I see it" approach usually signals more resistance than readiness for romance. Many women who adhere to this use it as an excuse not to date, thus avoiding MFDA. Their belief in instantaneous love eliminates any dating uncertainty and risk taking on their part.

I (Dr. C) would like to point out that when people can't tolerate the uncertainty of a dating situation, they focus on a projected fantasy of an idealized, *perfect* meeting with a *perfect* person, which results in a *perfect* relationship. The need to know whether you've found love at first sight is an unrealistic scenario created to avoid a confusing and frustrating dating process. I refer to this as your "dating fantasyland." Practicing this is dangerous because you aren't seeing a man for who he is, but rather who you *want* him to be. You may be avoiding real dating situations because you've become caught up with finding your fantasy—or even worse, you may be projecting this idealization onto some guy you don't really know that well after just a few weeks. Ultimately, you're setting yourself up for disappointment once you realize that it may have actually been *lust* and not *love* at first sight.

The Prince Fantasy

Do you believe that you'll be going along with your fabulous life, following your passions and career, when a man will suddenly appear—almost out of the sky—and it's as if he was made for you? It seems that his sole purpose on Earth is to find and love *you*. Hey, it's not a bad fantasy, but still, it *is* a fantasy.

Are you one of those women we encounter so frequently who basically doesn't focus on finding love, having children, or even dating because you believe that by concentrating on other things, a perfect man will suddenly and unexpectedly climb up into your ivory tower and make everything great? Are you looking for a prince on a white horse who will sweep you away to a better life, rescuing you from dating, boredom, and loneliness? The *Pretty Woman* fantasy affirms that a wonderful man will simply show up one day and solve all your problems . . . even if you're a hooker with a safety pin holding your boot together!

Despite the fact that this is a very common dating approach, this is a textbook rescue fantasy. We've found that the women who typically employ this do so when they feel incomplete without a man and are desperately looking for someone to make them feel whole. Let me (Ryan) remind you that some men are attracted to women who need to be rescued because these guys are itching to "fix" something in their girlfriend's life or help her out of a mess. They want to fulfill the rescuer role because it gives *them* a purpose. Few of these men come to realize that their need to rescue a woman is tied to their own anxiety and avoidance of intimacy. (We haven't written the MMDA book yet, but it's coming!)

As a dating approach, the prince fantasy may work well for you in the short term because it does what any approach should: It reduces MFDA by offering you a process to follow. Unfortunately, even if your prince shows up on a white horse (and he's looking great with his long, flowing hair) and sweeps you off to a castle in the sky, you still have to get to know him, and you might not like him when you do.

Your romance should last longer than the two hours you spent with Julia Roberts and Richard Gere. You have to slow down and get to know a guy. Discover whether you have a similar sense of humor and if you enjoy his wit, intelligence, or prowess—and hopefully he has some of each.

Remember that toward the end of *Pretty Woman,* Julia Roberts's character admitted that she'd always wanted the fantasy but realized that she didn't want to be rescued in the conventional sense. When asked what happens after the white knight rescues the princess (in the movie, this is the final scene when Richard Gere's character shows up in a white limo), she replies that the princess then becomes the rescuer. I (Dr. C) want to highlight how we've seen this same experience time and time again with the couples we work with. The women who settle down with their projected fantasy prince eventually come to resent the men who need to *rescue* and *fix* them all the time because at some point, they want to be an equal partner. We don't recommend that you search for a prince, unless you're a princess who's living in fantasyland.

The Three-Date Sex Rule

If you're only interested in sex, then the three-date rule (that is, waiting until Date #3 to hook up) is probably a good rule of thumb, but if you're looking for something more substantial, then this isn't the dating approach for you. In this modern dating environment, many people rely on this rule to determine when the appropriate amount of time has passed before sexual intercourse can occur.

However, this reduces dating to a time investment. The belief is that after three dates, you have enough information about a guy, and now you can officially sample the goods. It's like going for a test drive before you invest any real feelings in a potential partner. This approach assumes that by Date #3, you'll know if there's enough chemistry to explore a sexual relationship; then after having sex, you'll be able to determine if there's enough of a connection to pursue a committed relationship based on the quality of your sexual compatibility. In terms of escaping symptoms of MFDA, this is moving into something quickly to reduce the uncertainty of an exploratory waiting period.

This approach also puts a lot of emphasis on the physical part of a relationship because it assumes that the greater the physical chemistry, the greater the relationship potential. With so many magazines teaching you all the "tricks" that will "blow his mind," it's easy to see how the three-date rule is reinforced. Many women staunchly believe that if they can satisfy a man sexually, he'll fall in love and want to have a serious relationship. These women think that if they work on their seduction skills more than their communication skills, they can get a man close enough to show him how special they are. If they're sexy enough, then men will surely want them. But the truth is that a successful relationship needs a lot more than a physical connection.

Relationships that are based on sexual chemistry alone are like milk—they have a shelf life. To think that after three dates you could know a guy well enough to "give up the goods" and allow him the pleasure of your most intimate self is off track from the reality of how relationships evolve. We think you can and should give it more time.

At this fast pace, you'll miss the subtlety and joy of special moments of physical expression. Do you remember when you were a teenager, and a boy you liked touched your hand for the first time? Can you recall the electricity you felt at the mere *expectation* of him hugging you or kissing your cheek? We think that these youthful romances were even more exciting because it wasn't a foregone conclusion that you'd be getting naked. On the

contrary, you looked forward to even the smallest indications of mutual interest.

The three-date sex rule strips these special moments and replaces them with a false cure for MFDA. When you're exploring dating and using physical chemistry as the barometer for relationship success, you may have the illusion of closeness that comes from being sexually intimate. However, you may be overlooking all of the other aspects of a romantic connection, such as trust, vulnerability, and the ability to communicate. Many women who use this approach are happy to have waited until the third date, but by the fourth date, they're often still left wondering . . . are they dating their guy, are they now in a relationship, or could he be seeing other women? And then the MFDA sets in deeper.

The Wait-and-See Approach

The reason why many women rely on this particular approach is because it offers (what they think is) a stress-free and directionless dating style where there's no real need for closeness during romantic exploration. This belief is based on waiting to determine whether someone is worth investing any time into while casually examining the potential for romance. Keeping everything undefined until there's definitive proof that you're safe to involve yourself in a relationship with a guy is the essence of "wait and see."

When entering what feels like an unsafe dating environment, many modern female daters carry an internalized fear of rejection or of getting hurt (fear-based dating) so using the wait-and-see method is a way to keep a safe distance. They assume that by observing potential from "afar," they'll avoid emotional harm because they can date without exposing their genuine feelings. We often hear a wounded dater say, "I want to know for sure before letting myself feel anything, because I don't want to go through another short-lived romance. To protect myself from making that mistake again, I'll wait and see if he's worth my time."

This involves waiting for *some* form of evidence to materialize that guarantees whether or not it's safe to date. The strength of this approach is that it prevents your past wounds from reopening. It allows women to maintain the greatest emotional distance from the possible source of hurt.

When dating a guy casually, hanging out, hooking up, just going along, or waiting to see where it goes and if it's worth it, you may find yourself in dating limbo where you actually want more but don't know how to move in that direction. When using this approach, there's always a question of whether the dating process will ever be defined—and ultimately, it never is, leaving you in a perpetual state of waiting and wondering.

What's the Solution?

Modern female daters need a reliable method of evaluating relationship potential before committing emotionally and physically. In order to capture "lightning in a bottle" without getting burned, you have to have certain skills. While chemistry and sparks can be instantaneous, and the temptation to act on that attraction can be overpowering, there are other factors to consider when deciding to become intimate with someone—namely, how to date a guy long enough to observe his true nature. This has to be learned because it's not innate.

You need the SW Method. There's a little known fact that all successful business owners know, which also applies to dating and relationships: The underlying structure—the foundation and the infrastructure—is what holds it all together. Businesses establish systems for organizational and structural purposes, and like a flourishing business, you need a systematic dating approach to help formulate the internal structure of your relationships. A great love needs a solid foundation because the *relationship is the structure that holds it all together.*

An ideal dating system would teach you how to pace the formative dating stages and provide steps to follow when transforming

raw attraction into something more meaningful. Luckily, you now have such a method at your fingertips!

Our Approach: The Stop Wondering Method

When you've finished reading this book, you'll have the SW Method at your disposal all the time. It's a systematic approach that will forever change your dating life and intimate relationships. In the following chapters, as our Dating 101 class progresses, you'll learn essential lessons such as:

   When to call the guy you like

   The internal structure of a successful relationship

   A specific definition of *dating* that teaches essential skills and really shows you how to effectively date (It's not enough to just define something, you must see it in context and be able to apply it in the real world.)

   Tools for working through your personal MFDA

   Strategies for overcoming the obstacles that get in the way of a new relationship

   Step-by-step dating guidelines (yes, even how to go on formal dates with more than one guy as you explore relationship potential)

   The best way to pace a new relationship

   How to turn a spark of chemistry into a roaring inferno!

We call our revolutionary approach to dating the Stop Wondering Method because it offers you a way to finally *stop wondering if you'll ever meet him.* We'll teach you a formalized method for meeting men and making smart choices that avoids the pitfalls of the casual dating environment. By putting the *date* back into *dating,* you'll enjoy the process as you develop the romantic relationship you've always wanted without the MFDA that once plagued you. Are you ready to stop wondering?

PART II

Your Solution

Chapter 4

The Stop Wondering Method

When you eliminate your MFDA using our comprehensive approach, you'll finally stop wondering:

- If you'll ever meet *him*
- When he'll call you back
- If he's into *you* the way that you're into *him*
- When you'll see *him* again
- If you're his girlfriend or just a hook-up
- When he'll change into the man you hope he is
- If he's dating other people
- If the relationship will last

The SW Method will drastically shift your relationship perceptions and experiences, and make dating what it should be: *fun*. Instead of rules to follow, we supply guidelines that will actually help you through the challenging casual dating environment en route to the lasting relationship of your dreams. Rather than tips, tricks, chains, and whips, we offer tools, techniques, and a powerful strategy.

Let's begin by introducing the governing principle of the SW Method: *Meaningful relationships aren't formed instantaneously but take time to grow and evolve. Just like all other developmental processes, they move through distinct stages with unique characteristics. The SW Method is an approach that is composed of formalized dating stages marked by significant shifts in perception and behavior.*

If you want long-term, lasting love, you have to follow the plan. There will be no cutting corners or racing through it. However, you'll be pleasantly surprised to find that each step along the way will be fulfilling and enjoyable—that's our promise to you, if you dedicate yourself to learning the process.

In order for you to fully understand the SW Method, we need to give you some background information: The SW Method is a "stage theory," a concept used by a number of academic disciplines. (Basically, a stage theory illustrates that development occurs in a set sequence of qualitatively different stages.) Psychologists, psychiatrists, and biologists all describe developmental processes according to the changes that occur throughout the course of various stages. Dating is very much a developmental process.

All stage theories are based on the following underlying assumptions:

    🍃   Each stage lays the foundation for the next.

    🍃   Everyone goes through the same stages in the same order.

    🍃   Each stage is *qualitatively* different—meaning that it has specific qualities that distinguish it from other stages.

    🍃   There may be lasting consequences if a stage isn't completed properly. (In other words, people who go from the first date to a wild weekend in Vegas should just cut it out!)

It's very important to complete one stage before moving on to the next; in fact, we've got to stress this point—*it's really, really important.* We'll help you with this because we're not going to just redefine dating and hand you a formalized stage theory (the SW Method), we're also going to provide a revolutionary way for you to *internalize* the dating process with a visual, symbolic system.

What Does Gardening Have to Do with Dating?

Do you like flowers? We do. To us, they're the essence of sexual energy—yes, *sexual* energy. In nature, pollination is the *real* birds and bees. Flowers are all about beauty, fragrance, and reproduction. On Valentine's Day, what do many women look forward to receiving from men? Flowers, of course. A bouquet seems to embody sensuality and heartfelt feelings; and there's nothing else that symbolizes love, sex, and beauty in the same way. Knowing this, we decided long ago to use the metaphor of a blooming flower as the backdrop for our lesson plans. Basically, the SW Method is built on the genius of the natural world. Through years of refining our approach to dating and intimate relationships, we've found that the transformation of a flower— from seed to bloom—is the *perfect* way for our students to visualize the stages of the SW Method. After all, this type of imagery is already infused in our everyday speech. Think of the expressions "You reap what you sow" and "Harvesting the fruits of your labor." Salespeople often talk about "planting seeds" when they refer to potential clients, and, of course, there are new ideas that "stem" from one another. Nature really is the best teacher.

When you look at a flower, you know that it didn't go from seed to bud overnight; it's the product of careful *cultivation* and *nurturing.* A seed's potential isn't visible right away. Rather, the results are slowly revealed over time as the plant sprouts from the ground and continues to grow. Think of dating as planting "seeds" that have unknown potential. Even with Mr. Right, there is *still* a long process of growth (cultivating and nurturing

the seed) that's essential for deepening the bonds beyond initial chemistry and attraction.

The process of cultivating anything in the garden, board-room, or bedroom requires specific techniques; and just as a gar-dener can teach you the secrets of a successful bloom, we're giv-ing you a method to nourish a loving *relationship* into full bloom. However, many of the women we work with are at first nervous at the idea of taking time to see how a romance grows. They want to know right away if a "seed" is worth their effort so that they can move on and avoid wasting time or emotional energy dating. Unfortunately, they're looking for something that they think should be instantly recognizable. Not so fast!

The problem with impatience and acting impulsively is sim-ple: If your seed has grown into a seedling, you now have a young plant with the potential to flower. For a while, it's still only a bud that hasn't yet opened its petals to the world. Should you try to force the bloom to open faster than its natural course? Can you cheat nature? The answer is *no*. Sure, you could build a greenhouse with high-powered lights and dump tons of Miracle-Gro on the soil to drastically speed up the process, but your flower would only survive briefly in this unnatural environment. More important, it may *survive,* but it wouldn't *thrive.* Are you willing (and able) to sustain the enormous energy it would take to maintain this flower? Is that really what you want for yourself? Do you want something that's so hard to grow—something that has been forced?

The same is true with dating. Many women find a guy and decide that he's "perfect," rather than taking the time to discov-er if true relationship potential is there. What usually happens next is that they invest a lot of time and energy into "making it work" with a guy they *just met*—á la Julie's numerous heart-breaks. They dive headfirst into a relationship instead of gradu-ally easing themselves into it. Then when they quickly hit the shallow bottom of the "relationship," they stand there, rubbing their head—and smoothing out their Jennifer Aniston hairdo—*wondering* what happened. Stop wondering and learn to cultivate your love's true bloom.

*We promise that if you follow the Stop Wondering Method,
there will be no more intense, but short-lived, romances.
You will finally be able to have the relationship
you've always wanted.*

Before *you* dive headfirst into the SW Method, we'd like to ask you to do a little bit of preliminary work. Think of it as about ten minutes of required reading before class is back in session so that we're all on the same page when it comes to the topics in our dating syllabus.

Since we talk about love as a growth process as opposed to an instantaneous bond, you need to familiarize yourself with some terms in the SW methodology. There are certain factors that are easier to understand and apply when viewing them through the lens of our gardening concept. It can be hard to remember the steps of a stage theory, but it's easier and more fun to look at it as a blooming flower. Are you with us? If so, you'll see that your "internal garden" (where your relationships develop) is just like any other garden, because there will be factors or conditions that will determine if love blooms or dies on the vine.

In this chapter, we want to highlight the seven essential factors that are responsible for a successful relationship, and then we'll quickly introduce you to the six stages that will help love bloom in your life—from a seed to the lovely rose that you anticipate receiving from your future lover (and eventual husband). These growth factors work in harmony; if you ignore even one, the chances for lasting love are diminished and may even be impossible. You might want to bookmark these pages, making sure to reread them when you're actually going through the stages of a relationship. If you're following the system and notice that something isn't working, it might be that one of the factors is missing, or perhaps your romance garden needs some tending.

"Romance garden"? Since you're not actually going to be planting seeds all over your town or city, we're going to show you a place where your relationship seeds *can* flourish. Your personal

romance garden is a specific, consciously designated place within you where you keep all of your past loves and every dating experience you've ever had in your life. It's in this "garden" where the new seeds you plant will be cultivated, and the relationship "weeds" that strangle new growth will be pulled. We believe that the following factors are necessary for a healthy, flourishing romance garden.

The Seven Factors

FACTOR #1: PATIENCE
Growth Element: Time

The SW Method is a foolproof approach to dating because it teaches you one of the most important skills you need for relationship success: *patience*. In our high-speed, technological world, however, this is a difficult concept to master. Of course, we've all been told that "patience is a virtue," yet despite this, Julie often thought, *Why should I wait for anything when so many things are available to me right now these days? I can't be patient because I'm running out of time—my clock is ticking, and the hour is almost up!*

We understand Julie's frustration but counter with this: Even though you may be able to instantly order your favorite shampoo online, that's not the way you're going to find a long-term, intimate relationship. You can't order *him* via overnight delivery; love doesn't arrive at your doorstep in a tidy package. This is why cultivating patience is so important, and it touches on one of our favorite principles: *You can't get to tomorrow any faster, so you must learn to live and love the moments of today.*

That's easier said than done, right? Yet patience is crucial for love because the inner calm, peacefulness, steady perseverance, and the ability to suppress restlessness allow men to become captivated by you. Let me (Ryan) put it plainly: Men hate the full-court press or feeling like a woman has an agenda. But when a woman is patient and isn't needy of a man's attention and affection, it makes him curious about her. Impatience is your worst enemy because it communicates desperation. Guys love to be challenged by women who don't immediately fall into bed with them. Sure, men *like* a quick pounce every now and again, but we *love* to feel that what we have is prized. We learn early on in life that hard work is the key to success, so if sleeping with someone comes too easily, most guys assume that it must not be valuable. When a woman we desire forces us to be patient, it turns us on.

This is why guys don't put in a lot of effort when a girl is calling them all the time (which you know results from MFDA). On the other hand, they're intrigued and want to get to know the woman who communicates (through her actions) that she is calm and confident. Patience is an attractive quality and a very important factor in the SW Method. Later on you'll also see that pacing a relationship (exercising your patience) is the key to female empowerment. By tuning in to your internal timetable, you'll also eliminate impulsive behaviors that are caused by MFDA.

This is powerful stuff because it enables you to be fully present in each moment with self-control and the capacity to tolerate waiting for the unknown. Answers in love will be revealed in time. As your mother may have said, "Good things come to those who wait."

Within the romance garden, the corresponding "growth element" is time. Once you've carefully planted your seeds, you must be patient while they grow. If you attempt to cheat nature and speed things up by constantly adding fertilizer, you risk destroying new growth by burning out the roots, or you'll end up with something that takes so much *unnatural* energy to sustain it that it won't survive for very long. When things ripen slowly in their own natural time, you'll grow the most fragrant and beautiful flowers.

Factor #2: Flexibility
Growth Element: Resiliency

"Hey, I know we had a date at 5 P.M., but are you *flexible?*" This word is used so often that it feels meaningless and uninspired, but the truth is that flexibility is a crucial skill that must be developed. If you're able to bend and flow with life's changes and challenges, you won't "snap" like so many others do when dating.

Being flexible means that you're able to adjust to the unexpected events that life can sometimes throw at you without cracking or falling apart. In dating, this concept is huge. Let's say that you've envisioned a clear picture of Mr. Right. But what happens if you meet him and he doesn't exactly fit your image of perfection? Uh-oh . . . what happens when reality doesn't match your fantasy? Maybe his greatness is within him in ways that aren't immediately noticeable. Is it possible that it could still be great—maybe even better than you expected? Are you flexible enough to explore something that may have amazing potential but can only be revealed over time?

Have things happened in your life that had been much different from what you thought they'd be, yet still ended up being great? The power of this trait is being able to accept *and* adapt to the unknown. You need to be open and less rigid when it comes to exploring new romantic possibilities that don't match your ideal because the reality is that things rarely show up exactly as expected. Being flexible is essential because what you may have imagined about your true love (a six-foot-tall blond), may actually arrive as something different—a guy who's 5'6" with brown hair . . . or no hair! What happens now? Does your MFDA cancel the order and send him packing? Or is it possible that you could be flexible enough to explore whether he can change your mind?

You may still be holding on to old images of what you think you want or who you should be with based on what your parents or friends have told you over the years. But when you're open, you're able to see possibilities that you've never imagined. On the other hand, it's also important to know how flexible you can be because all things have a breaking point—even huge trees topple under the right wind conditions. You'll learn to discover *your* breaking point because, of course, there will be some things that you can't be flexible about—and it's vital to understand and acknowledge these pressure points.

The corresponding growth element in your romance garden is resiliency. When a plant is resilient, it can bend and dance in the wind without damaging its stem or snapping. Hardy plants can survive severe weather and remain upright even in adverse conditions. Like nature, relationships can be unpredictable; sometimes storms blow through without much warning. But when the harsh conditions subside (and they usually do), if you've been resilient and adjusted to your environment you will have made it through without too much trouble.

FACTOR #3: MYSTIQUE
Growth Element: Air

There are many ways to describe a woman who possesses mystique: She's charismatic and alluring; she's magnetic and has an electrifying personality; she exhibits grace, exuberance, positive energy, joie de vivre, and charm; and so on. It may seem that you must be born with this trait, but we don't agree. Our particular use of the word is a tad different. For us, it simply refers to a *personal quality that attracts or captivates others.*

Mystique is an essence: It's something you experience but can't really see—in the same way that you breathe in (but don't see) the air around you. Plants take in carbon dioxide and release oxygen into the environment, cleansing the air we breathe. Like plants, we require fresh, unpolluted air. Imagine what would happen to a garden that was placed in the middle of a factory where

the air was blackened with thick smoke. But the same garden would flourish in the country where the air was pure and intoxicating.

Men will either have a positive or negative experience with the "air" (or mystique) you exude; they won't quite be able to put their finger on why they feel a certain way, but they feel it. Guys say that when they encounter a woman with mystique, it's captivating and makes them feel more alive and energetic. A woman with mystique makes others feel good. People are drawn in and say things like, "She's a breath of fresh air."

What specifically is the benefit of having mystique? Well, a person with mystique in a dating situation projects calmness, confidence, authenticity, and focus. She almost always possesses superb communication skills, too. These women naturally attract many more suitors and will have many more dating options. That's reason enough for most women to consciously develop and reflect these characteristics.

The most surprising aspect of mystique is that it ultimately has *nothing* to do with outer beauty; it's an internal quality that can be far more of an aphrodisiac than a pretty face. I (Ryan) know for a fact that when men are looking for a relationship, they'll actually gravitate to a less attractive woman who has that *special something*. Yeah, men see a pretty face, and that attracts them on a physical level, but if nothing else but a great beauty is present, we get bored. Men want substance—believe it or not—and as I can attest, all men remember being intrigued by a woman's mystique because its effect lasts longer than bedding a "perfect 10."

That *special something* makes all the difference to the men you're interested in, and we're going to teach you how to be more attractive by developing and maintaining a charismatic "air" that other people will respond to instinctively. You'll learn how to create a powerful aura that attracts (and thus makes you more attractive to) the men you desire.

In the romance garden, the obvious corresponding growth element is air. In your garden, we're referring to the seemingly empty space that surrounds the flowers—the invisible atmosphere between the fence and plants, even the spaces between the leaves. Of course, we know that a garden can't flourish if the atmosphere is dirty and polluted, so we'll show you how to maintain the air quality in your inner garden. Basically, you need to make the air that surrounds you (between *your* leaves and limbs) fresh and clean and free of negative thoughts! Let the air that you carry be warm, refreshing, and clear.

When an individual has an air that is foul smelling and polluted, you know it the minute he or she enters the room. And it's obvious when someone carries an "air of superiority." We'll show you how to monitor the air of the people around you, too, because some may have hidden pollutants. Guys you're dating (or will be dating) have their own masculine mystique—make sure their air doesn't stink.

Factor #4: Boundaries
Growth Element: Room to Root

Boundaries allow you to be yourself because they're the borders that you enforce and maintain in your life. Let me (Dr. C) explain what we mean by this: Boundaries refer to the emotional and physical space that exists between you and another person; they denote the *limits* of *self* and *other*. When they're crossed, it's natural to feel discomfort because your "safe space" has been violated. However, your personal boundaries shouldn't be rigid, as they can and should change based on how intimately you're connected to a person. When it comes to dating, establishing clear boundaries is very important because they define who you are as a modern female dater. Without words, they reflect *how you date* to the men you meet, showing them where you stand, if you'll go home with them on the first night, whether you want to see them again, or even if you'll give them your phone number.

One of the biggest mistakes people make is failing to enforce any boundaries for fear of frightening away a potential lover.

There's also a tendency for some to dissolve borders and merge with their partners—whereby they've become one beating heart with no lines of delineation between them.

It may seem romantic to get lost in one another, but we don't think so. An indication of this is when every sentence is started with the word *we:* "We like baseball," "We love the color red," or "We don't like him." Although some merging is healthy and indicates a strong attachment, complete enmeshment is *not* healthy and doesn't signify a balanced relationship. This usually happens to a woman who doesn't have a strong sense of self and ultimately defines who she is according to the man she's currently dating.

Signs of this include feelings that you *should* do everything together and be perfectly aligned in all ways. There's even pressure to like the same things because differences cause discomfort in the relationship. Although meeting and falling for the man of your dreams may feel like you've found your other half, the truth is that letting someone else actually "complete" you is dangerous.

Just as there may be a tendency to merge too early in the dating process, there are also those who feel extremely uncomfortable with closeness and want to keep others at a distance. They are *very* aware of their personal boundaries and can feel suffocated or afraid of getting hurt when their partner gets too close. These boundaries are more like a ten-foot-tall concrete wall than a charming fence at the edge of your property.

We'll show you how to establish your dating boundaries while exploring a developing relationship. It's empowering to establish clear, well-maintained boundaries that allow you to become close to someone yet also maintain your individuality. Let me (Ryan) explain the guys' perspective: Men want women who can be independent, especially during the initial dating periods. Women who want to get lost in love can be frightening. We may want to move fast, but *we want you to make us move slowly.* The guy you're seeing may really want to get in your pants, but at the same time, he also wants you to stop him. Men like a woman who has boundaries because they make her seem slightly unattainable, which you should be. A man has to be *invited* into your garden—he can't just hop the fence and come in as he pleases!

In addition, we always tell our clients that losing yourself in a relationship is dangerous because when you no longer exist, men will look for something else. With boundaries, you're declaring that you have your own life and are busy cultivating other seeds of potential.

The corresponding growth element for this factor is "room to root." As seeds expand and become flowers, the roots need space to spread out and anchor into the soil. If two seeds are planted too close together, the developing roots may wrap around each other, choking both plants—or even worse, creating a situation where one dominates the other. Establishing healthy boundaries outlines your personal space and makes men respect you and your dating approach. If they don't, then that tells you something about them and who they really are inside.

FACTOR #5: INFORMATION
Growth Element: Nutrients

Even though you probably never attended a formal dating class—until now, of course—you've internalized tons of information about dating from every conceivable source in your surrounding environment. Throughout the years, you've absorbed various teachings on "the art of the pickup" and "the game of love." Your friends, family members, and the media have consistently been your biggest influences; and over time you've filed away the data and subconsciously factored it into your dating patterns, choices, and overall mind-set.

The danger of having all of these "teachers" is that you can get conflicting information. Many women still think it's harmless to read tabloid magazines while standing in line at the supermarket or to watch every episode of *The Bachelor*. Guess what—it's not! Even though the women we work with insist that they don't really take that stuff seriously, they're unaware of just how much

these images and ideas influence their thoughts, feelings, and behaviors. Although it may be fun to watch the romantic chaos of your favorite celebrity(s) unfold, like it or not, your subconscious is absorbing everything you see and hear on TMZ, which deeply influences the choices you make and how you experience *your* dating environment.

For instance, take Julie's mom, who is a six-time divorcée and offers relationship tips to her daughter all the time. Unfortunately, her advice is based on her own failed marriages, so Julie probably isn't getting the best counsel from Mom. Hopefully, your mom offers better insights than Julie's!

In the absence of a formal dating education, reality TV has become a powerful teacher of love and romance. I (Dr. C) want to point out that even though many people might think that these reality shows are meaningless entertainment, on some level, they're experiencing what they see as truth. Viewers are bombarded with images of supposed genuine reactions from real people in real situations; as this information is imprinted in their subconscious, it inevitably affects their search for love. Let's not forget that these shows are a lot more scripted than they appear— that is, they enjoy the power of editing. As a result of this distorted influence, many women begin to look and act in similar ways because they start to believe that it's what men want. Just by watching romantic pursuits on TV and in movies, real women subtly pursue similar paths and then expect to have a neat, happy ending at the conclusion of the episode (their date).

It's time to go back to the garden for a little while. The corresponding growth element for information is nutrients, which provide a plant with the nourishment it needs. When there aren't adequate nutrients—or the wrong ones are present—the earth isn't fertile and can't support new growth. By looking at the information you consume as various "nutrients," you can easily see how you have to be careful about what you put into your soil if you want your flowers to be healthy and flourish. Don't let acidic nutrients creep in—unless, of course, the plant you want to grow needs acidic soil!

The same is true with dating: Be selective when it comes to the information you consume, and don't allow corrosive nutrients into your soil.

FACTOR #6: EMOTIONAL AVAILABILITY
Growth Element: Water

A relationship requires emotional investment, but how much and how soon are the questions that must be addressed. There tends to be consensus among all the men and women we've consulted with over the years, and according to the majority, emotions are the lifeblood of relationships. Without blood in your body, you'll die; without emotions in your heart, you'll die alone.

That's a frightening thought, considering our belief that life is all about love and happiness. These emotional states are revered and sought after by people worldwide—across language barriers and cultural divides. Emotions are the most dynamic aspect of a relationship because they make up the feelings and deep-connecting agents—the glue and bond. This is why when you first begin to date a guy, you need to assess your *emotional availability* to determine whether you're able to openly engage with him while exploring relationship potential. If you bring a healthy, clear state of mind to the dating process, you'll have a source of emotions that are at your disposal when the time for intimacy is right. You'll have established a genuine and deeply fulfilling bond between the two of you. That is no small task, however.

The SW Method will take you through the dating stages, and each one will require greater emotional investment. I (Dr. C) want to stress that developing an attachment for someone and having strong feelings should happen slowly over a period of time because the ability to modulate your emotional investment indicates relationship readiness. So at the start of the dating process, you must ensure that your emotions are in your control and at your disposal.

We've watched beautiful, educated women throw their emotions wildly at men, thinking that it makes guys feel more strongly because they now *know* how deeply a woman loves them. No, sorry, it doesn't work that way for men. I (Ryan) know that this kind of emotional vulnerability scares most men to death because for us, deep feelings come very slowly and cautiously. We aren't encouraged like women are to be *in touch with our feelings* and expressive with our emotions. Wild emotional involvement can be flattering, but ultimately, it's overwhelming. Later these women are stunned when their guys head for the hills or look like they want to be swallowed into the earth.

Is a man who won't share his feelings a jerk? Well, he could be, but it could also be a reaction to your overwhelming emotional outpouring too soon that derailed the relationship's potential. You'll never know what could have been because you didn't take the time (patience factor) to get to know him and ended up scaring him away. It's not your fault if you've been prone to this type of behavior, though; no one showed you how to regulate your emotional investment. Emotional availability influences *how* and *whom* you date. Know that it's okay to date just "for fun," especially after a painful breakup or divorce. But you've got to understand the difference between casual dating and dating with direction and purpose. If you're following the SW Method, you must be clear about your ultimate intention: Do you want to have a good time or find true love? If your answer is to find love, then you must be open and honest about your emotional availability.

The corresponding growth element in your internal romance garden is water, as it is commonly used to represent the flow of emotions. Think of the expressions "treading water," "drowning in debt," being in "hot water," and "boiling mad"; these watery references describe strong emotional states. In the garden, water is vital for plants to make and process nutrients. How often you water (tune in to the flow of your emotions) depends on a lot of things. Without a gardener to teach you, you may not know how to water properly—and without water (or with too much), your plants will die. However, there is a method, and it takes knowledge and skill to know when and how much water to give your romance garden.

Another important aspect of this is the *source* of your water. Think of it as a well that stores and houses water with an easy-access bucket. The image of a well is synonymous with another common aspect of water: the idea of *soul water*. When the well is full and overflowing, you have plenty of water at your disposal (you're emotionally available), but when it's dry, it's like having no tears left to cry. Is your well filled up and easily accessible?

Just like the air aspect of the garden (that is, your mystique), beware of polluted water. Make sure that yours is clean and fresh, ready to be gulped down when you're thirsty. Testing his "water quality" is also a way to gather information while dating (more about that later), because his soul water needs to be abundant and clear so that he's able to cultivate his own garden and possible love with you. You can't compensate for a guy who has a dry well, so make sure that the men you date have their own source of emotional availability.

Remember the old saying "Still waters run deep"? This implies depth in an individual, which is sexy, but be careful not to drown your plants just because you have lots of water (emotional depth) at your disposal. This is a great image for our students and consultation clients because many women can more clearly see the dangers of "overwatering" their budding relationships. They begin to understand how too much emotional investment too soon can ultimately drown the seeds and young plants before they can establish firm roots.

In your internal garden, you need to closely monitor how much you water your seeds. Be aware that if you're overwatering due to fear and panic, the relationship will drown. We'll show you how to properly water throughout the stages of the SW Method.

FACTOR #7: FAITH
Growth Element: Sunlight

Faith is a tricky word because it conjures up religious or spiritual beliefs that provide comfort to some and discomfort to others. Our version of faith is open to your own interpretation. We just want to introduce the notion that an internal belief that love is possible is crucial for a relationship to succeed.

Regardless of how you view the source of this life-force energy, we want to show you how to have faith in the face of heartbreak and years of loneliness. You should have faith that there's perfection in all that has happened and will happen as you step into the unknown. You should have faith that love exists in a special realm and comes into your life from an unknown, uncertain tomorrow that brings with it new possibilities. We believe that love is a spiritual journey of the highest order; whatever your basic belief system is when speaking of faith in the SW Method, we're simply acknowledging *an inner knowing* that some *force of energy* is working on your behalf. What's the benefit of faith in love? If you always know that you can tap into the gift of this faith energy when you need to, you'll always have an anchor when an emotional storm blows through your life.

You might personally find this source energy through the spiritual (God or otherwise), the metaphysical (the universe), or of scientific origins (mathematics). Ultimately, it doesn't matter; what matters is that those who don't have any source of faith are often cut off from having a loving relationship because they deny themselves access to those energies, which may exist beyond what's seen and experienced by the physical senses. Take a chance and use the power of your faith to allow a new love to enter your life like never before.

We've come to the final corresponding growth element in the garden: sunlight. In order to grow and create food, plants need the sun's powerful rays; otherwise, they'll wither and die. In addition, some plants require full sun and others take partial shade, so you must know how much energy is needed for each individual seed variety.

Can you see how important faith is in the dating process? We believe that it can be a powerful tool for you to utilize when you understand how much energy is required to grow the perfect seed to its ultimate potential. If you deny your faith, you're choosing to grow with no sunlight at all.

Your Romance Garden

By applying these factors, you'll learn how to grow relationships according to nature's purest principles. And as you follow the stages of the SW Method, you'll learn how to cultivate each seed (potential relationship) gathered (from dating) and how to nurture a plant that blooms year after year (a long-term, committed relationship).

In addition to helping you develop the seven factors, we'll teach you methods for gathering seeds (involving Internet dating, meeting men at bars, and more), planting them (going on dates), correctly watering (nurturing the relationship), and then choosing which seedling has the most growth potential. As we move along the process, you'll see how this method will help you confidently move from casual dating to an intimate relationship.

To really illustrate this process, we encourage you to do something that many of our students participate in. We recommend that you plant some seeds in a small terra-cotta pot on your windowsill. This is fun because it offers you a tangible representation of the growth process that you'll be experiencing in your dating life. You'll be able to cultivate (by adjusting the growth elements) an actual flower seedling that will constantly remind you of the growth sequence you're following in this book.

Whether you decide to start with a seedling or a mature plant, you'll still learn how your care and intimate connection can blossom into the relationship you've always wanted. And the good news is that even if you're already in a relationship or involved

in the dating process, *this book is also for you.* You can apply these growth principles to your current romantic relationship and yield beautiful flowers. Let us explain some more: Are you currently dating a guy and are unsure if the situation has real potential? Or maybe you're having some trouble in your existing relationship and are looking for some new insight. Perhaps you'd like to increase current levels of intimacy and work through some of the stages that you may have missed.

Whatever your motivation is, we're excited to give you a snapshot of what's to come. The following is a brief description of the six stages of the SW Method that we'll explore together:

Stage One: Your Ideal Man

SW Speak: Seed Selection

Objective: Envisioning a clear picture of the ideal man you want to date and the relationship you desire

Stage Two: Preparing to Date

SW Speak: Doing Groundwork

Objective: Getting ready for a new relationship by creating a positive dating mind-set

Stage Three: Looking for Love in All the Right Places

SW Speak: Gathering Seeds

Objective: Attracting men you may actually want to date

Stage Four: First Dates

SW Speak: Planting Seeds
Objective: Beginning to date; determining if there's enough potential to go on a second date; and deciding whom you'll be dating

Stage Five: Exploring Relationship Potential

SW Speak: Cultivating Blooms
Objective: Exploring multiple options through a formalized dating process

Stage Six: Entering a Committed Relationship

SW Speak: First Bloom
Objective: Deciding which dating option has the most potential and then choosing that man for a committed relationship; working together to sustain a deeply fulfilling, intimate connection

Chapter 5

Stage One: Your Ideal Man

We want to offer you our heartfelt congratulations for demonstrating *patience* (you're still reading, aren't you?) while allowing us the *time* to lay down the groundwork before getting to the heart of the SW Method. So let's dive in and determine what kind of relationship you want and, most important, with whom.

This is indeed the good stuff because you'll envision your ideal man and your relationship with him. What could be more fun than having no limits in creating the perfect guy? This stage is focused on getting really clear about how you want your love life to look in the future. There are *no boundaries* here! When you fully describe your truest desires and leave behind what others may have said you *should* look for, your ideal man will actually be able to show up in your life sooner than you ever thought. Even if you believe that you already know the kind of relationship you want, we don't recommend that you skip this stage. In this chapter, we're going to help you refine that vision while determining if your ideals reflect realistic desires.

On the other hand, if you find yourself in a situation where you have no idea what you really want or perhaps have come to realize that what you *used* to want no longer fits your life, consider this your clean slate. Through years of working with our various clients, we've found that defining and articulating a romantic vision in very clear terms is crucial. (Plus, if you know what you're looking for in the first place, it will certainly be easier to recognize him when he shows up!)

Your Ideal-Man Checklist

Your Ideal-Man Checklist is an anchor to hold on to when you're being pulled by the many confusing signals of the modern dating landscape. This list prevents you from losing your way by giving you a comprehensive and categorical group of ideal attributes.

We know a few women who've written their lists on their favorite stationery and keep them in their purses at all times for emergencies. This is now true of Julie, who met Darren, a very hot guy who wanted to take her home the first night they met, insisting that their chemistry was "insane." Rather than immediately saying yes, however, she excused herself and went to the restroom. She pulled out her Ideal-Man Checklist, which reminded her that she'd met many Darrens in her lifetime, and now she wanted someone different. After consulting her trusty list, she went back to the bar, said no to Darren, and gave Tom her number instead! Just like in Julie's case, your Ideal-Man Checklist can keep you from getting scattered or falling into old attraction patterns.

There are subtle dangers involved in making a list without guidance, and most women who have done so in the past have come up with several expectations that have been practically impossible to meet. Some of the women we've counseled have been envisioning the perfect man in their minds for years without refining or altering their desires based on new life experiences. When using the list incorrectly (creating unrealistic, unreasonable standards), women might set up criteria that no one man can meet, as no one is ever good enough. Someone's list might even be more than ten years old, yet it has never been revised! Interestingly, setting too high expectations is usually due to an avoidance of true intimacy, which is a reaction to MFDA. This is a defense against vulnerability and fear rather than an attempt to fall in love. However, a flexible, realistic list offers women a chance to see in straightforward *words* the images and ideas that they may have been pondering for years.

We don't want you to sit down and write that he must be rich, handsome, and have a three-picture deal at Warner Bros. Think about the real traits that you long for in a mate: Perhaps he is kind and strong during a crisis and doesn't fall apart. Maybe he's the type of man who dreams big and doesn't allow minor setbacks to sidetrack him. As you create your list, reflect on your past dating experiences. For instance, maybe your last boyfriend had a hair-trigger temper and now you definitely want someone who's able to manage his anger.

Visualize Your Ideal Mate

Visualization is a technique that involves becoming clear about, and "seeing," the positive results that you're hoping for in your life. Most people use this tool to achieve success in their business endeavors or for personal growth, but we do something quite distinctive: We turn the tool toward love. We believe that if you want to give yourself the best chance of relationship success, it's important to choose wisely from the start. How many times have you seen intelligent women fruitlessly trying to *make it work* with the wrong guys? Before going on a single date, you need to ask yourself some preliminary questions to determine what the ideal relationship you envision *really* looks like.

So let's explore and fantasize. Don't just say that you're "looking for love," which is true but doesn't go deep enough. Too often love is mistaken for lust; you need to be as specific as possible during this process.

Remember Josh—Julie's "rock star" fling in college? He wasn't a terrible person, but he definitely wasn't a good match for Julie. At the time, she thought she could change him and turn him into what she wanted. She'd complain to her girlfriends that he was irresponsible, and she started to resent the fact that other girls would hang all over him at gigs. Hello! What kind of seed did Julie find in the first place? She looked for the seed packet that said "wild rocker type"—and that's what she got!

Look into your future and see that beautiful dream. It's fun to take some time and really get into it because you're reconnecting with your inner child—but instead of dreaming about being a ballerina (or a veterinarian), you're envisioning a wonderful romance that fulfills your heart's desire.

When it comes to selecting a life partner, this is an *empowering* act. It's about you and nobody else!

SW Speak: Seed Selection

Let's go back to your romance garden. As most gardeners know, the secret of a plant's life is locked in its seeds, which contain the genetic material needed in order for anything to grow. When you buy a tiny packet of seeds from your local nursery or market, you have an idea of what they're going to look like when fully grown.

Seed selection is the first growth stage because it involves planning for what will happen down the road. Keeping the seven factors in mind, start visualizing the types of "seeds" that you'll plant in your romance garden. Let's begin to generate some of that genetic seed material now so you can form a clear picture of what you're looking for in a mate.

What Are You Looking for in a Mate?

On a separate piece of paper, or on the note pages at the end of the book, complete these sentences as honestly as you can:

I imagine that my perfect guy would love to do things like _____. When we're together, I want him to treat me _____. My vision of myself in this relationship is that I feel _____ when I'm with him. It's important to me that I'm able to talk with him about things such as _____.

At first, it may be difficult for you to fill in the blanks. But whether or not you feel this way, here are some additional questions to help you define your ideal man. Ask yourself:

1. *What do I want from this man that I don't currently have in my life?*

2. *What would he do to make me happy?*

3. *What would be different about me if this perfect guy was in my life?*

Perhaps you're looking for someone who will expand your horizons, learn with you, grow with you, and love you. What kind of man will fill that bill? Some women want a guy who is gallant and not prissy; able to cry, but not too soft; polite, but not a pushover; or tough, but not overly aggressive.

Here's a list of the most important qualities that a man should possess, according to our clients:

 A good sense of humor

 The skill to communicate intelligently and openly about subjects such as art, politics, personal thoughts and emotions, relationship issues, work issues, and so forth

 The ability to make you feel safe and/or protected when you're with him

 Trustworthiness and compassion (someone you can reveal your true self to—that is, being vulnerable, crying, showing uncertainty, and so on)

In addition to an ideal man's characteristics, our clients also stated that an *ideal,* loving relationship should include:

 Dynamic sexual chemistry

 Shared common interests

 Similar values and purpose in life

 The desire to introduce each other to the significant people in your lives

 The ability to enjoy silent moments together without discomfort or anxiety

 Similar goals, lifestyles, and visions of the future (that is, you're both walking the same path to the same destination)

While you're visualizing your perfect love, we caution you *not* to focus too much on physical attributes. Yes, it's fun to think about your ideal man looking like Brad Pitt—which he might—but it won't help if it causes you to limit your possibilities for love if he doesn't resemble a sexy Hollywood celeb.

You must practice flexibility and explore the far reaches of your breaking point to discover how important the external is in relation to the internal. What if a guy you meet has almost all of the characteristics you desire but looks different from how you envisioned? Will you dismiss him? We have a client who informed us that she only likes men who have blond hair and wear little round glasses. That's her "type," as she described it, and she'd only entertain the thought of a relationship with a guy who fits the bill. Unfortunately, she wouldn't recognize a great catch if he was standing right in front of her!

A few years ago, our client did meet her ideal man. She was ecstatic and immediately "knew" he was the One. They went out for three months, but then she slowly discovered that he was a workaholic who valued business success more than creating intimacy with his partner. Despite this, she dug in and insisted that he was the perfect man for her because he fulfilled her physical fantasy, and she was willing to settle even though she knew that he'd always value his work first. Many perks came from his success, but she sacrificed having a truly loving relationship.

At the end of the day, if life is about love and happiness, what do hair color and glasses have to do with anything? Love has nothing to do with physical beauty. Inner traits such as trustworthiness, compassion, and wanting to create a life with someone are essential in forming lasting, loving relationships. Certainly, physical attraction is important, but it also changes over time. In addition, we know that when you like a guy's personality, he becomes even more attractive to you.

At this point, you might have preferences when it comes to physical attributes—and that's okay—but we're asking you to keep an open mind, because love comes in many shapes, forms, and yes, hair colors, too.

What Traits Should Your Ideal Man Possess?

Choose 20 of the following attributes (both internal and external) that would describe your perfect man:

Intelligent	Honest	Stylish
Generous	Trustworthy	Vegetarian
Passionate	Sensual	Lean/thin
Polite	Adventurous	Older
Sophisticated	Family-minded	Younger
Educated	Muscular/stocky	Debonair
Funny	Tall, dark, and	Radiant
Vulnerable	handsome	Independent
Well-endowed	Laid-back	Carefree
Preppy	Health-conscious	Humble
Rock-star chic	Rugged	Extroverted
Businesslike	Metrosexual	Old-fashioned
Liberal	Articulate	Friendly
Conservative	Witty	Introverted
Artistic	Hedonistic	Aloof/cool
Romantic	Spiritual	Charismatic
Family man	Outdoorsy	Fit/athletic

Take some time to think about your personal list to ensure that it accurately describes the ideal traits that you'd be thrilled to find in a guy.

Do You Have a Type?

Think about it: Do you have a type? Because you're envisioning your ideal romance, it's important to look back briefly on whether you've spent a majority of your dating lifetime believing that you have one specific type when it comes to love. Relationships that didn't work out in the past could be related to this as well. Do you think that your answers to the questions in the previous exercises could have been influenced by your old beliefs?

There's a good chance that you've been pursuing a version of your type for years (even if you've done this subconsciously). Have you always been attracted to men with dark hair and light-colored eyes? Do you feel drawn to athletes or cowboys? Perhaps you've always loved the rougher, macho guys, or you might gravitate toward those who are quiet and seemingly shy and bookish. Is there a certain emotional type that seems perfect for you—someone who's emotionally available for love?

Have you ever *really* found your type? Was he all that you'd hoped for? Did anything fall short? Have you ever had a real emotional relationship with your type? Perhaps the answer is yes, and if so, congratulations. We're the last ones who would place limitations on anything, and there's no question that you may have encountered your type and had success with him. What we're getting at is this: A *type* tends (for the majority of women we've encountered) to represent a fantasy man, who's nothing more than an idealized image generated in your brain at a young age. This pattern of attraction is formed early in life and is subsequently pursued repeatedly over the years.

Why Do You Love the Men You Do?

Let's look deeper at the root of what caused your attraction to certain men. Think about whether your type is really your *own* description of the perfect guy. How or when was it formed? Does it accurately reflect a deep knowledge and awareness of what works in your life based on your own experiences? Or maybe your father pushed you to find a rich executive; or your mother told you that the strong, silent type is the best. If not, maybe you've been looking for a guy who's like your father.

Starting early in life, you've been slowly mapping out the path of your current love life. Since you were a child, you've been forming your attractions. We want to talk more about the con-

cept of "mapping" because it holds the key to your dating past and future.

Edward C. Tolman, an American psychologist, was a brilliant man who's generally credited with introducing the term *cognitive map*. Basically, he explains that people use mental models (or belief systems) to perceive, contextualize, simplify, and make sense of otherwise complex problems. A "lovemap" is a similar concept that was conceived by John Money, who used it to explain why individuals like what they enjoy sexually. According to Money, a lovemap is a "developmental representation or template in the mind and in the brain depicting the idealized lover and the idealized program of sexual and erotic activity projected in imagery or actually engaged in with that lover."

We'd like to introduce our concept of the "intimate map" in the SW Method because it helps us explain why you find certain individuals attractive and what causes you to pursue romantic relationships with them. Understanding this is essential because it will help you create your ideal man by including new possibilities that will enlarge your dating pool.

Your intimate map has been shaped by both positive and negative experiences. There have been things that have attracted or repelled you as your intimate preferences were being subconsciously charted. We want to look at these with you right now so that you have an idea of what you've mapped thus far (and why) and how it has affected your dating choices.

All of your romantic experiences over the years have been plotted on your intimate map, which affects the types of connections you've formed (and will form) with others. You can't expect to break old patterns if you don't carefully examine how they became your patterns in the first place. The points of interest on your map show up as a group of messages encoded in your brain that describe your likes and dislikes, including your preferences in hair and eye color, voice, smell, and build. Your map has also recorded the kind of personality in a guy that appeals to you.

What are we getting at here? You fall for and pursue those people who most clearly fit your intimate map, and as we stated earlier, this image is largely determined in childhood. Let me (Dr. C) add this: Did you know that by the time you're eight, the pattern for your ideal mate is already in your head? You already have a preliminary lovemap; in fact, the guy you're interested in now probably has traits that are similar to what your mother likes in a man. Maybe your mom married someone who is strong and brave—it wouldn't be unusual to realize that you're attracted to the same traits. If your mom likes a guy who is more brainy, you might also prefer that type.

Your mother was the first love of your life (for most children) and certainly the center of your world as a child. It follows that your mom's choices and actions in love would leave an indelible impression on the choices *you* make. In addition, you've probably been attracted to people who have similar facial features, body type, personality, and even sense of humor as your mom. And if she is warm and giving, you tend to be attracted to people who are also that way. Think about the messages you learned from how she approached *her* life. You may want men who are nothing like what she desired, but even that has a powerful impact and impression on your intimate map.

While your mother may determine in large part what qualities you find attractive in a mate, it's your father (the first male in your life) who greatly influences *how* you relate to the opposite sex. Fathers have an enormous effect on their children's personalities and chances of marital happiness. Let me (Dr. C) elaborate: Your dad also has a say here, and he really influences the type of guys you like. Let's say that as you were growing up, your dad was very supportive and always told you how smart and creative you were. You are more likely to naturally feel good about men. But maybe Dad was always criticizing you. In this case, you may feel unloved or even ineffectual around men.

The good news is that this isn't permanent. Your intimate map can be changed; your journey thus far only represents where you've been up to this point. With new information and a willingness to keep an open mind, your path can even be redirected—it *is* possible to chart new territory!

 **Wondering . . .**

The key to dissolving limiting relationship patterns is to understand why you started to think this way in the first place. You may continue to be attracted to a certain "type," but as you become more aware of how you mapped this ideal, you'll realize that just because a person looks or acts in a certain way, it doesn't mean he has what it takes to have a great relationship with you. You may find that you're open to other possibilities that you've never noticed in the past because they hadn't been previously mapped.

Once you're aware that it's a particular experience with one of your parents that has led you to believe that *all* men are a certain way (or do certain things), you may be open to seeing them differently. It's not possible for all men to be one thing or another. It's important to figure out who a guy really is before you show him to the door.

Let's take a look at some of the factors that have helped shape your intimate map so we can continue to refine your list. Before you fully realize what you want from a man *and* a relationship, you've got to dig deep! (We're standing by with shovels.)

What's Your Type?

Take a moment and ask yourself these questions:

1. *I would describe my type as* _____.
   [Try to think of as many characteristics as you can; use the previous questions and exercises to guide you.]

2. *When I think back, it seems that my attraction for this type started when* _____.

3. *Some of the people or factors that influenced my type are* _____.

4. *My ideal type resembles one or both of my parents in this way:* _____.

5. *My mother and I are both attracted to someone who* _____.

6. *My father treated me like* _____. *That made me feel* _____ *about men.*

7. *Other men probably will treat me the same way because* _____.

8. *Other men will probably treat me differently because* _____.

It's helpful to view your type as an idea that needs refining. You might never meet someone who fills every aspect. He might be handsome but not financially stable, or he has a great job and a bit of a belly. One of the keys to romantic perfection can be found in loving someone's *imperfections*. This is illustrated in the film *Good Will Hunting* when Robin Williams's character gives a lovely speech about his late wife. He said that he loved her deeply and for many reasons, including the fact that she often passed gas in her sleep. We're just guessing that when he was envisioning his ideal woman, it wasn't one who exhibited this charming quirk.

Your shortcomings are what make you unique, and it's best to shut off your fantasy version of a man and realize that there's no such thing as perfection. *There's only perfect for you. If someone is right for you, they're perfect <u>with</u> their imperfections.* In fact, it may be people's quirks or faults that you come to love most about them.

You also have to consider that the original type you mapped out long ago might not be truly compatible with you. If you're a city girl who has a high-powered career in New York City and you're in a long-distance relationship with a cowboy who works the land, this attraction might stem from a fantasy based on a Wild West romance novel you read as a teenager. Are you sure your lives could mesh? Sure, it's possible if you look beyond the rugged exterior and discover that his internal characteristics also fit your ideal. Look beyond the "type" to discover if he's perfect for *you*.

If you think you'll *never* meet your type, you should ask yourself if you're subconsciously choosing men you'll never meet. Why would anyone do that? You must become aware if your map causes you to *purposely* be attracted to a type of man who's unattainable, because this signifies that you aren't really ready or available for love. For instance, when the CPA with the big heart comes along and you aren't willing to consider dating him because your type is a wealthy CEO—even though you never actually meet any wealthy CEOs—you may be selecting a man you'll never find to avoid the risk of being hurt or let down.

Does your map indicate a type of man who truly meshes with your lifestyle? If you want to date a jock but prefer to sit in the house and watch movies, then something is wrong on a compatibility level. One of our students loved the image of an outdoorsy man in a dirt-stained tank top, carrying his kayak over his muscular, tanned shoulders. When she met an actual kayaker online, everything seemed incredibly romantic until they had their third date (on a river), and he was disappointed to discover her fear of water! She realized that he was too gung ho for her, and ultimately, her fantasy didn't fit her reality. She needed to refine her search parameters.

Chemistry

When we talk about being compatible, simple surface tests may come to mind, but they don't really indicate a deeper connection with a guy. For instance, just because you like camping and he does, too, it doesn't mean that you're going to be married for 50 years.

A lasting relationship is based on much more than just attraction and some mutual interests. Attraction tends to be a spark that only indicates potential; chemistry, on the other hand, is a deep connection that unites lovers in an emotional *and* intellectual way. True chemistry doesn't equate to love at first sight because chemistry (genuinely bonding with someone) takes time. Attraction can be instant, but this alone isn't love—it's lust!

Refining Your Ideal-Man Checklist

Take a moment to go back to the questions posed earlier in the chapter and your list of attributes. Go through them again and see if anything has changed, knowing what you now know about your intimate map and type. Are there any changes, additions, or subtractions to your initial list that you want to make? Remember that this is the template for your ideal mate. Take your time and make sure that it actually reflects your desires and intentions.

Back to the Romance Garden

In the garden, we talk about this part of the process as the time when you're in a nursery deciding what types of plants you want to pick up. At this point you ask yourself, *What do I want? What do I like? What will grow well in my soil?*

If you've gone through the process successfully and you've looked at your type and are clear about what you value in a man, then you already know the answers to those questions. You must remember, however, that many flowers don't look anything like

the seeds they came from in the first place. Beautiful, exotic buds often have an unattractive appearance at first—only becoming beautiful as their potential is revealed through the growth process. Seed selection isn't about finding an exact blueprint of your revised checklist; it's about using a broad list of attributes, keeping them in mind, and then finding men who embody some of those characteristics.

Perhaps the seed you find (the next guy you end up dating) is a little different from what you imagined. The important first step is that you need to be flexible. You don't really know what you'll find because there are no "man seed" stores! You have to get out there and gather the seeds.

When beginning to meet various men—in coffee shops, on the Internet, through friends, and so on—you have to constantly remind yourself what you want and require in a mate. Consulting your list helps you remain clear and open to new types of men, because inevitably you're going to plant some seeds that are by their very nature designed for dating practice only. Not all seeds will grow, and not all men will have boyfriend potential.

Look deep into the genetic content of the seed variety and discover what's inside so that you can envision what type of plant you've got on your hands. Don't write a guy off just because he likes to camp and you're an uptown girl who needs a four-star hotel. He can camp with his friends once in a while, and you can go to a spa with your girlfriends! If this same man is spiritual, creative, loving, and full of joy, that's much more important than the fact that you won't live in a tent and eat granola a few weekends a year.

True love takes time to reveal itself—so be *patient.* Stop living your tomorrow like it was your yesterday. Live each day as if it's the first moment of your new life and you don't know whom you might meet or what amazing thing might happen. Trust and practice your *faith* using the rationale that certain people come into your life in unexpected ways. Don't be afraid to open your eyes and embrace the unknown.

A Quick Story (We Love) on Love

We worked with a woman whose family owned a huge Western-wear clothing company. She had a distinct idea about what type of seeds she wanted to plant and was convinced that there was no way to deviate from it because she knew what attracted her. She told us, "I want a Wild West type—a real rugged guy who spends his days on the land and loves the open trails. I've never been attracted to anything other than this kind of guy. I can't help it; it is what it is."

She refused to date a man if he didn't fit that requirement because she grew up around horses and loved to roam the woods on the weekends. She wouldn't even imagine that she might meet a guy who could learn to love those things if given the chance. We asked her to dig deeper and figure out what attributes she really liked about this fantasy seed. She responded that her ideal man is adventurous, courageous, and a little wild. We asked if she would be willing to see if there were other types of men who had those traits even though they weren't cowboys. Could she find those qualities in a writer or a doctor?

Well, as it turned out, there was a man who worked in the shipping unit of her family's company. He was a rugged guy who could lift a building, but he didn't grow up horseback riding. He'd asked her out months ago, but she completely blew him off—that is, until a few weeks into her seed-gathering process when she mentioned to us, "Oh, yeah, this guy at work expressed interest in me recently."

So while working with the SW Method, she decided to give him a shot. We encouraged her and said, "Hey, you never know! You might have fun, so get back in the saddle, and maybe you'll find your ideal seed later on down the road. But just enjoy the dating process. You never know until *you know more about him,* and you don't have enough information yet."

In a very casual way, she talked to him the next day and even apologized for virtually ignoring his suggestion that they could go out for a drink sometime. She said, "I'm sorry that I never said yes,

but I'm around this weekend and thought maybe we could get that drink." (Simple. Easy.) Usually we don't advise a woman to ask out the guy she's interested in because we believe that the man should do the initial asking (more about this concept is coming).

Well, they did go out for that drink and had an amazing time. She even admitted to superficially judging him at first and realized that he was actually really smart and very good-looking when cleaned up. They ended up dating according to the SW Method and eventually entered into a committed relationship.

Eventually, she realized that he wasn't her happy ending and they didn't stay together, but through the process she really learned how to enjoy dating again. This was a huge breakthrough for her, and she started opening herself up in new ways that she'd never before thought were possible. Suddenly she wasn't looking for just a cowboy hat. At a bar, she'd actually glance around the room to see who was really there. She learned to send clear signals that indicated interest, and before long, men began to ask her out like never before.

She continued to refine her seed-selection process and eventually found a man who wasn't a cowboy at all, but loved the rodeo and had the *spirit* of a cowboy. (He also didn't have the reckless, distant qualities that many of her old cowboy flings had in the past.) This guy had a great job, and they were able to travel in the summer to the Calgary Stampede rodeo in Canada. Ultimately, she ended up with someone she didn't expect and wouldn't have even considered if she hadn't refined her seed selection. By the way, they got married and are expecting their first little buckaroo!

In the end, don't chase a fantasy. Sure, it's great if he looks like Usher and sparks wildly fly, but it's not so wonderful if two months later you're *wondering* what happened because you have nothing in common (plus, you suspect that he's using you for work contacts). However, there are countless stories where two people meet and don't think they're each other's type, but it's just electric between them. They take the time to get to know one another—building the chemistry between them—and they're usually the ones who end up happily married for 30 years.

A Special Word If You Just Broke Up with Someone

We want to say one quick word to women who've just gone through a breakup or a divorce. It's very easy to go out and look for seeds that are just like the person who just checked out of your life. But we urge you not to follow this template, even though it's tempting to duplicate the situation you've just lost. The new man won't look like or *love like* the man who was there before. Don't settle for someone just because you sense a resemblance, which may be comforting initially.

Another one of our students dated a really great guy for three years who looked like Antonio Banderas. They broke up, and before long she found someone else who had a similar look, but instead of another nice guy, he was a big jerk. Yet she was determined for this new seed to bloom so he could fill the space left by the one who'd left her. Please avoid this trap, because trying to clone a past relationship only causes more hurt and resentment. Also consider the fact that your new love doesn't want to be a replacement player—you wouldn't want to be one either.

There are even some women who date men who resemble their ex-husbands because they feel as if they've transformed the old relationship by applying a fresh coat of paint and making a few other "repairs." Again, attempting to upgrade what didn't work in the past isn't going to make it work beautifully now. It's just an unhealthy fantasy. Instead, create your ideal-man checklist, and find someone who possesses those traits.

Are you ready to find your ideal man? Now you know what you want (and why), but before you start gathering some great seeds, you have to do more work on *you*. So let's get busy!

Chapter 6

Stage Two: Preparing to Date

Before we delve any deeper into the SW Method and begin looking for men to date, the time has come to stop and ask an important question: Are you sure that you're even *ready* to date? If so, are you ready to *really* date in a way that incorporates the Four Pillars of Intimacy? Do you want to experience passionate love, mind-blowing sex, and a dynamic long-term relationship through our formalized dating method?

Typically when we ask our students this, almost all of them immediately respond with: "Of course I'm ready to date! I want to find my true love, and I'm ready to do whatever it takes." That's wonderful enthusiasm, but this excitement doesn't necessarily indicate readiness.

We strongly believe that you can only succeed in this dating process if you're willing to fully engage and do everything it takes to have a successful relationship. Before going any further, think about whether you're ready to date in a new way—one that involves

setting clear intentions and following through each of the six stages with purpose, which is the objective of the SW Method.

Are you able to change your old dating habits and restrictive patterns? If you answered yes in your head as quickly and easily as some of our students have, then we'll also emphasize that you need to slow down, take a breath, and tune in to your inner knowing.

Ask yourself, *Am I <u>really</u> ready to date?*

This is important because many of the women we come in contact with have been wounded by past dating experiences, yet they continue to jump from one unhealthy relationship to the next. Often these women are feeling lonely and desire companionship, but because they haven't done any inner work, they continue the cycle of dating defensively. Instead of believing in love and having *faith,* they're stuck thinking that they'll never find someone as good as old "what's his name"—"the one who got away." Some of them firmly believe that "chivalry is dead" and that "there are no good men out there."

We want you to consider whether you're truly open to new dating possibilities. Or are you perhaps like some of the women we've worked with who say they're ready but are also convinced that many factors beyond their control are sabotaging their romantic success, such as "I'm too old to date," "All the nice guys already have wives/girlfriends," "The guys I like don't go to bars," and so on?

Within the SW Method, this mind-set is seen simply as encompassing limiting thoughts that need to be removed—*nothing more, nothing less.* If you recognize yourself here, you're suffering from MFDA and need to work through it. Limiting thoughts have to be dealt with *before* you start dating to ensure the greatest success. In other words, the problem might not just be the *type* of men you're dating, but may also have to do with your negative thought process.

Back to the Romance Garden

Let's visit your internal romance garden, where your true love's bloom will be cultivated. In SW-speak, the second stage is called *doing groundwork* because no seeds can be planted until the ground has been properly prepared. Many untrained gardeners believe they can just throw seeds into some holes and everything will magically bloom . . . not so!

Would you plant a bunch of rare seeds in rocky, claylike soil even though you knew that they'd have practically no chance of growing? If you had an exotic seed in your hand, wouldn't you take into account its requirements for healthy growth while making sure that the soil was in ideal condition?

Soil provides a nutrient-rich growing environment for seeds to germinate and blossom. If your internal "soil" (your dating mind-set) is overwhelmed with weeds, they must first be pulled; and if your soil has been drained of vital minerals, these must be replenished. Your soil holds everything together and allows for the greatest probability of success. An experienced gardener knows how important this step is for long-term growth. In order to cultivate dating seeds that will flourish, you must have a fertile mind-set. If you're not open and ready to sustain a new relationship, then no love will bloom. Instead, your soil will remain a rocky and lonely outcrop.

So . . . are you ready to supplement your soil?

Are You Ready for a Relationship?

An important factor in the success of any romance is readiness—meaning that you're available to open yourself up to another person in a committed, focused way. Whether or not you're able to find that special someone isn't solely the result of blind luck; it's also largely determined by your reasons for wanting a significant other in the first place. In order to know if you

are indeed ready, you must be very clear about what motivates your search—that is, aside from wanting love, what are your other reasons for desiring a mate?

Perhaps you think it's time you settled down because your biological clock is ticking. Or maybe your parents are pressuring you to "get a real life" (meaning a house, kids, and a two-car garage). Is it because many of your friends are in relationships and you're tired of being a third wheel? There are many women out there who spend their nights curled up with the remote control in one hand and a diet cola in the other, desperate to be saved from their loneliness.

For example, Julie can't stand the idea of spending yet another Friday night at home watching *Friends* reruns on TV. She'd much rather meet someone—anyone—in order to enjoy a more exciting life and certainly to perk up her weekends.

Do you want a boyfriend simply for what he can or will do for you? Do you want a special someone because having a relationship will fill you up and make your life more meaningful? We don't think that settling into a relationship for these reasons is the best way to set yourself up for ultimate love and happiness. If you need a mate for external reasons, such as getting to the next economic rung or because it will make your family happy, then you have more digging to do in your romance garden.

There are myriad motivations that drive people to want a relationship, and it's important to look at and try to understand their reasoning. I (Dr. C) want to mention a key research study performed by psychotherapist Emily Kensington when she asked 100 couples the following question: "What do you love most about one another?"

If the answer indicated little depth or revelation about the internal being of the other person, the relationship was generally considered to be shallow and often didn't last very long. For instance, replies such as "Because she's pretty" or "He's fun" were negative predictors, revealing surface attraction that usually led nowhere fast. But when couples listed reasons such as

"She's compassionate and trustworthy" or "He understands me deeply," the results reflected long-term, successful relationships.

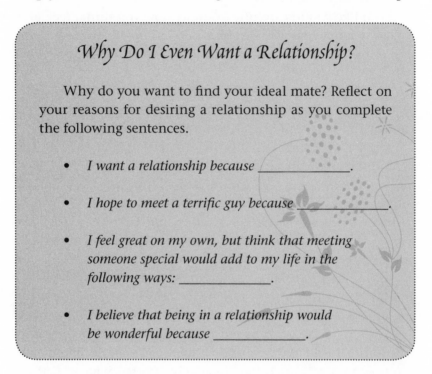

Why Do I Even Want a Relationship?

Why do you want to find your ideal mate? Reflect on your reasons for desiring a relationship as you complete the following sentences.

- *I want a relationship because* _____.

- *I hope to meet a terrific guy because* _____.

- *I feel great on my own, but think that meeting someone special would add to my life in the following ways:* _____.

- *I believe that being in a relationship would be wonderful because* _____.

There are certainly internal *and* external reasons that drive the desire for romance, but according to the study that I (Dr. C) mentioned, these external reasons are the least predictive of relationship success. When you're unhappy with some aspect of your life or yourself, you may look to another person or to a romantic relationship to "complete" or fulfill you.

The idea that another person can complete you is very dangerous! It implies that you're not whole on your own and that you're invested in the relationship in a way that may foster *dependence* rather than *partnership*. If this rings true for you, you aren't ready to start dating yet. But all hope is not lost! The objective of this stage isn't to jump headfirst into a relationship; we want you to do your inner groundwork and positively transform your dating mind-set.

 **STOP** *Wondering . . .*

Doing Groundwork

We'd like you to carefully examine how you think, feel, and behave when it comes to romance and dating. If you have negative, unrealistic, and limiting thoughts; if you're emotionally unstable; or if your behavior seems out of control at times (these are all manifestations of MFDA), then you'll stunt the growth of potential relationships before they get started—without even knowing it.

The soil of your internal garden represents your current dating mind-set—the place where you hold all of your beliefs, feelings, and experiences regarding love. Each romantic relationship you've had was planted and has grown (or died) in this soil. Think back to your earliest romances. As they ended, did they leave you with rocky soil (a negative mind-set) or fertile ground (a sense of possibility about what was to come)?

As any experienced gardener knows, the soil must be tilled and infused with nutrients after each season. So now we want you to look at your internal garden and think about how many times you've tended to your soil after a breakup. Did anyone help you do this work? We've already established that no one taught you how to date, which has negatively affected your soil. Who showed you how to care for your romance garden after each relationship ended? Is your soil still fertile after all these years, or is it barren?

What has taken root in your garden? Think back and recall whether you've grown beautiful roses or wildflowers (which you didn't really want or plan for in the first place). Perhaps you grow the same flowers again and again even though they never bloom the way you'd hoped. Do you wish you could plant something different but seem unable to? Maybe your soil (your mind-set) is preventing you from doing so.

Looking at your inner garden in this way represents an important stage of self-discovery, as you may now realize that you have infertile soil that hasn't been tilled for years, or your garden may be infested with weeds and overgrowth. You may even have wild, untamed flowers (booty calls, unrequited love affairs, and so on) that are still growing even though you claim to be ready for a deeper relationship. If you're still cultivating these types of relationships in your garden soil, it's time to find out if they need to be removed or tended to, with the intent to help them bloom.

Digging Deeper

Take a moment to dig deep within yourself, and answer the following questions:

1. Are there any old relationships that are sucking the nutrients from your soil, preventing you from growing anything new?

2. Do you find that you've grown the same kind of relationships again and again?

3. Do you feel unable to plant something different in your garden?

4. Have you been trying to grow new seeds without success?

5. Is there something in your garden that you continue to water (with your emotions) once in a while? Is it just clinging to life and not allowing anything else to grow? (This could be an ex, the memory of an ex, or a "friend with benefits" who drains your well and depletes your soil's nutrients.)

Exploring Your Personal Dating History

Let's examine how the past has influenced and formed your current dating mind-set. As we demonstrated, every romantic experience, thought, and feeling has influenced your "soil"; therefore, the quality of future relationships is dependent on your upkeep. We know it's not always fun to get up in the morning and tend to your garden. Sometimes it feels like work—and it *is* work, but it's so worth it. Remember the saying about enjoying "the fruits of your labor"?

It's time to grab a rake and start tilling your soil. You don't have to be a kid to enjoy digging in the dirt!

How Your Past Relationships Have Affected Your Garden's Soil

Now is the time to think about your past relationships as you fill in the blanks in the following sentences:

1. *When I think about the time I was most heartbroken in my life, I remember being sad because _____.
I decided that I'd never date again because I never wanted to have _____ happen again.*

2. *When I think of my earliest dating experiences, I wish that I'd known how to _____ better.*

3. *My biggest dating mistake was when I _____.*

4. *A mistake that I keep repeating is _____.*

5. *The most positive dating experience that I can remember is when I _____. I try to still _____, but it doesn't always work.*

---

6. *I should have never gone out with* _____
   because _____.

7. *He reminds me of a few other guys I've dated,*
   such as _____. [Do any names come to mind?]
   They all have this in common: _____.

8. *I'm so happy I dated* _____. *He's the kind of guy*
   I'd want to date now.

9. *I wish my relationship with* _____ *had gotten*
   more serious. It didn't get serious because _____.

10. *If I could go back in time and do something*
    different, I would have _____.

11. [Think back to your most painful breakup.]
    That relationship didn't work out because I
    _____ [think of three things you did that
    you believe led to the breakup], *and because*
    I'm _____ [think of three things about
    yourself that probably made him not want to
    have a relationship with you].

12. *When guys break up with me, it's usually because*
    I _____.

13. *When I break up with a guy, it's usually because*
    he _____.

14. *Based on my past experiences, I think the reasons*
    why I haven't been successful at dating are _____.

15. *Sometimes I'm afraid to put myself out there*
    because _____.

How was that for you? Are you wondering why we made you dredge up the past in this way? Let me (Dr. C) explain: Whether or not you even remember all of your experiences, they contributed to your current dating mind-set. Even if this is the first time you've thought about these things in years, this tilling of the soil helps you reevaluate past relationships and prepare for new ones.

All that we're asking you to do right now is think about your influences and understand how they formed your intimate map. So let's keep digging, shall we, because we were just getting to the good stuff.

What are the various nutrients that affect your soil's fertility? Throughout your life, you've gathered information and messages from numerous sources outside your personal dating and relationship experiences. It's important to discover whether these factors have promoted or discouraged growth. Let's take a closer look at these influences, starting with your friends.

Your Friends

From your earliest memories, you can recall having fun with your friends, who grew with you over the years as you shared experiences together. As you began dating—and since no one was offering any formal instruction—you often learned from your friends and modeled your actions and choices on what you saw them doing. You may have copied your friends' dating styles because it looked like they worked or because you wanted social approval. Your friends have been endless sources of advice; whether or not they knew what they were doing, they always believed that they knew what was best for *you*.

Even though long talks with your girlfriends about guys can be fun, feel good, and can even pacify you (temporarily), the reality is that their advice won't often help in the long run because they need what you need: a comprehensive dating system. Without making serious changes to how you interact with men, you'll continue to commiserate with friends while all of you suffer from MFDA.

How Your Friends Have Contributed to Your Dating Mind-set

When I think of my earliest dating experiences . . .

1. *I dealt with competition with other girls by _____.*

2. *I cared what my friends thought of my boyfriends because _____.*

3. *I felt _____ when close friends were in relationships and I wasn't.*

4. *My friend _____ was always great to talk to about guys because she _____.*

5. *The best advice I ever got was _____.*

6. *When I'm upset about a guy, I always tell _____ first because he/she is _____.*

7. *_____ is a good friend who can always see positive qualities in the person I'm dating.*

8. *_____ is my most critical friend. He/she can always find something wrong with the person I'm dating.*

9. *My friends always told me that I _____ when dating, and that I'd be more successful if I only _____ more often.*

10. *I secretly think that _____ is happiest when I'm single.*

11. *When I'm single, I'm most uncomfortable socializing with _____.*

12. *I only socialize with _____ when I'm single.*

13. *_____ is a friend who gives me advice and has a great romantic relationship.*

14. *_____ is a friend who gives me advice and has a lot of trouble with his/her own dating life.*

15. *_____ has the kind of relationship I want.*

Wow! You have to admit that completing those sentences gives you some indication about how your social environment has drastically affected your dating mind-set. As you can see, your friends have had a profound influence on your dating life. They've been your sounding board from the very beginning— your own personal therapists without degrees!

In fact, your friends have a vested interest in your love life and feel that they know you best and what will work for you. It's admirable for your friends to want to help you (and vice versa), but they aren't really able to offer clear, unbiased advice. You may have even realized (after answering the questions in this section) that some friends might prefer it when you're single and can be very critical of the guys you date. If your best friend is lonely, she might secretly (or unconsciously) want you to be in the same lonely boat. The point is that many friendships aren't supportive of dating.

Getting dating advice and information from friends is a mixed bag because it depends on *their* experiences. Remember that the tips they're dispensing originate from their own dating mind-sets. Do they have any weeds or limiting thoughts in their romance gardens?

Yes, it's true: Friends *can* give each other great advice and insights about communication and what to do on a date, but it can be spotty on a case-by-case basis. Just remember to take their dating advice with a grain of salt. The most beneficial thing you and your friends can do is to help each other stay on track with the SW Method so that none of you ever loses your way again.

Your Parents

Just like your friends, your relatives also have a profound effect on your dating life—they may even have a greater influence because they're involved in your earliest experiences. Mom and Dad have shaped your views, but at the same time they haven't had any dating training either, so when they're involved in the choices you're making, they won't be able to offer much help.

We know that sounds harsh, as many women have wonderfully supportive and loving parents, but that doesn't mean they know how to date and form successful relationships. Whether your parents are still happily in love or are each on their fourth marriage, their advice about men can't really guide you as you navigate through this complex dating environment.

Indeed, parents (and other adult role models and guardians) have helped shape your core beliefs about love. What were the strongest parental messages you received when you first started to date? What guidance are you getting from your parents these days? Even if they've passed on, can you recall some of their insights? Perhaps your mom urged you to find a boy who was funny or romantic; maybe your dad wanted you to marry a doctor or lawyer. Did your parents ever state that if you dated someone who didn't practice their religion, you would be disappointing them on an epic level? As you can see, they've probably been very invested in (and vocal about) your dating life and are unable to offer objective advice.

Julie is very pretty, but her looks have nothing to do with successful dating and relationship formation. In fact, at the age of 13, she was emotionally scarred by an upsetting experience when she and her best friend were arguing about a boy. Her father overheard the fight and sat her down later in the day after her friend had left.

He said, "Jules, don't be jealous that Marnie has a boyfriend. She's a beautiful girl, and the truth is that boys may like her more now than they like you. But you're so smart, and one day boys will see how great you are." Julie was a late bloomer and still feels inadequate when it comes to men being attracted to her. *MFDA, anyone?*

At first glance, it seems like her dad was just trying to be helpful, but the wounds he unknowingly inflicted with his simple comment have plagued Julie her whole life. How has this affected her mind-set, and what weeds fill her garden? Well, she always seeks approval and validation from the men she dates. No matter how attractive she is, she still doesn't feel pretty and believes that she has to constantly compete with her friends for the attention of men. And regardless of how many guys approach her, she never feels good enough. This insecurity causes her to act impulsively because she's so anxious (MFDA) to know if a guy is interested.

Even though your parents instill thought patterns that stick with you for life, you *can* remove those limitations by taking care of and tilling your soil.

How Your Parents Have Contributed to Your Dating Mind-set

Think about how your parents have shaped your beliefs on love and relationships, and complete the following sentences:

1. When it comes to dating, my mom always told me _____.

2. Even if she didn't say it, I knew my mom wanted me to date someone who was _____. I knew she felt this way because _____.

3. When it comes to dating, my dad always told me _____.

4. Even if he didn't say it, I knew my dad wanted me to date someone who was _____. I knew he felt this way because _____.

5. From seeing my parents' relationship, I learned that love is _____, and you should always _____ and never _____.

6. Based on my parents' marriage, I know that a relationship involves _____.

7. I feel optimistic that I'll have a good marriage because my parents taught me how to _____.

8. I'm worried that I'll get divorced because _____.

9. Sometimes my boyfriends remind me of my mom when they _____.

10. Sometimes my boyfriends remind me of my dad when they _____.

11. A negative quality that I see in my mother _and_ the men I date is _____.

12. A negative quality that I see in my father _and_ the men I date is _____.

We hope this exercise helps you identify how your parents have shaped your beliefs. Over the years, strong messages and flawed ideas about love and relationships have been deeply imprinted in your mind, but don't lose *faith* because you can uproot negative family habits, and separate out the useful information for cultivating your nutrient-rich soil. How can you do this? Hang on for a moment . . . we'll tell you everything you need to know about "pulling weeds" once we've finished discussing your major influences.

Your Siblings

When you were a teenager, you probably didn't care what your dorky brother or sister thought of your love life, right? Or perhaps a sibling has always been an amazing role model and mentor. Either way, just as your parents do, siblings also deeply impact your dating mind-set.

Growing up, you watched them and learned from their mistakes, and they may have even pulled you aside from time to time and taught you their tricks of the dating trade. Siblings play an important role because they're often able to openly communicate with each other in a way that parents, teachers, and even friends can't. However, did they always know what they were doing when it came to dating?

Julie learned about dating at the tender age of 12 from her older sister. Even now she can recall her sister's simple approach to getting a boyfriend: "All you have to do is flirt with a boy you like, and try to make him your boyfriend." If only it were that simple!

The information you've gathered over the years has helped you formulate each dating strategy for every guy you've dated. Your brother or sister may still be your sounding board, but a sibling can't offer you objective advice any more than your mom or dad can. Have you ever been told to "dump that jerk!" because "he'd never fit in with our family." Do you really want a sibling calling *your* dating shots . . . even now?

How Your Siblings Have Contributed to Your Dating Mind-set

Think about how your siblings have shaped your beliefs on love and relationships, and complete the following sentences:

1. *I care what my siblings think about my boyfriend because _____.*

2. *It's important that my boyfriend gets along with my family because _____.*

3. *When it comes to dating, compared to my siblings, I'm the one who always _____.*

4. *My siblings would describe my dating life as _____.*

5. *The best advice my siblings ever gave me was _____ because it showed me that I can _____.*

Can you see how much your siblings have influenced your dating life? The things they've said and done are a part of your essence. In order to move forward and have the type of love you desire, you have to be committed to trusting *your* instincts and your teachers'—meaning *us,* in case you didn't know!

 Wondering...

The Media

The media is a tricky beast when it comes to dating. We're going to devote some time (and a few thought-provoking quizzes) to this subject because the media has a powerful influence on your beliefs about love, dating, and sex. Famous relationships among Hollywood stars have become the models that many women subconsciously follow. In addition, you're constantly bombarded with myriad advertisements that teach you what's sexy and which perfume will drive him wild. This source of conflicting information is the most polluted and dangerous of all.

In many ways, the media has given you a "positive" mindset about dating, because you've seen on TV (or in the movies) how it happens. You've watched when people fall in love, what it looks like, how to find it—and that it's all so easy. How many times have you seen a movie with this plotline: love at first sight, followed by a tiny snafu that creates a huge misunderstanding, and then (drumroll, please) the heartfelt revelation that they really love each other in the end? And they all live happily ever after. . . .

In real life, it's not so easy, and it takes more than two hours to find true love. In fact, it takes much more than making eye contact with a handsome stranger across a crowded room! In this manner, the media corrupts your perception of love and happiness, which can result in a negative mind-set about dating. Despite this, we still enjoy movies, TV, magazines, books, radio talk shows, and all those billboards featuring sexy couples who are seductively gazing at each other behind a spectacular sunset in the background. Watching (or listening to) all of these influences can be fun, a real turn-on, and even humorous. Plus, sometimes you might just want to believe that it can be so simple. Again, this illustrates the danger of the media: It cleverly presents gigantic dating myths that you desperately want to be true.

How the Media Has Contributed to Your Dating Mind-set

Think about how the media has shaped your beliefs on love and relationships, and complete the following sentences:

1. *The most powerful messages about dating that I've observed in the media have told me to_____ in order to be successful with men.*

2. *The most powerful messages about love that I've observed in the media have told me that it's something that _____.*

3. *The most powerful messages about relationships that I've observed in the media have told me that _____ is involved in any successful union.*

4. *The most powerful messages about sex that I've observed in the media have told me that _____.*

Hopefully you're starting to see just how much the media has programmed unrealistic messages into your dating mind-set. And, believe it or not, you've actually learned dating behaviors from Brad and Jen, Brad and Angelina, Jen and Vince, and so on. On a conscious level, you're probably aware that what you've read in gossip mags is exaggerated and often deceptive, but on a subconscious level, your expectations are subtly being shaped. And when your experiences with the men you date don't match these expectations, you'll suffer some serious disappointment (and MFDA)—which continually reinforces your negative dating mind-set.

Think about it: The media is *filled* with images and messages about the single life being glamorous and exciting. Jetsetting around the world, attending fabulous parties, and constantly changing partners might be a pastime for your favorite celebrity, but is that really your ideal lifestyle—and would you want it to always be that way?

What about the chemistry and connection of a dynamic relationship? It's usually *not* found in a whirlwind Hollywood romance.

How Hollywood Celebs Have Contributed to Your Dating Mind-set

We've discussed how the media in general has influenced your dating mind-set. Now we want you to think of your three favorite celebrity couples, and complete the following statements:

1. They seem like a good couple because they _____.

2. He probably chose her because she is _____.

3. She probably chose him because he is _____.

4. They've been together for _____ months/years.

5. Would I like to have a relationship just like theirs? Why or why not?

Messages about Sex in the Media

Not only did you learn about dating, love, and relationships from the media, but you've probably received *most* of your Sex Ed from Carrie Bradshaw, Bridget Jones, Monica, or Rachel. Do those names ring a bell? In those characters' dating lives, they usually had way too much casual sex that didn't lead to fruitful relationships. (Just watch the reruns of *Sex and the City* and *Friends* as a reminder.)

The media is filled with false layers of sexuality, and your beliefs about sex and love have inevitably been shaped by the images you've been exposed to all of your life—there's no way around it. You could probably name ten movies (in ten seconds) that contain passionate love scenes with dim lighting and sultry music.

You've been taught two distinctions:

— **Casual sex** is guilt-free pleasure that takes place spontaneously between attractive strangers and casual acquaintances. It's portrayed as erotic, passionate, reckless, impulsive, fun, and forbidden. (See Samantha on *Sex and the City.*)

— **Romantic sex** is what people usually think of when they hear the word *romance,* and it usually includes candlelit rooms, elegant dinners, and dreamy vacations. This is the only time we see foreplay on television, and it's portrayed as gentle, loving, and sometimes very passionate. (See all those episodes of *The Bachelor.* Of course, those five minutes of romance lead to a quick hop in the sack and then a swift kick off the show. How romantic!)

Once again, although it may seem silly, these images really do contribute to your dating mind-set.

Sex and the Media

What specific messages about sex have you learned from the media? Think about this as you complete the following sentences:

1. *A whirlwind romance followed by a wedding in an exotic location sounds _____ to me.*

2. *When I see the women on The Bachelor (and other reality shows) competing for a man, I feel _____.*

3. *The biggest lesson that I learned about sex from the media is _____.*

4. *Sex in the movies usually happens this way: _____.*

5. *I feel good about my choices compared to what I've seen on TV because I'm _____, and I believe that sex is _____.*

6. *I feel bad because compared to what I've watched on TV, I'm _____.*

Now think of a celebrity for each of the following: *I wish I could . . .*

- Look like _____.
- Dress like _____.
- Be like _____.
- Date like _____.
- Have a husband like _____.

What Are Weeds?

Oh goody, we love this part! In your romance garden, in your soil, all the limiting thoughts that interfere with dating and get in the way of new relationships are represented as weeds. Any gardener will tell you that weeds are a nuisance and can destroy a beautiful garden if they aren't managed. Not only are they unattractive—beware, however, some weeds pose as flowers—but they also compete for sunlight, water, and nutrients, as well as cause root crowding. They can strangle the life out of a budding seedling.

Weeds limit everything in your romance garden. As you're preparing your soil, you must examine your own weeds—those that are deeply rooted in your psyche. There are weeds you've had for years, and ultimately, it doesn't do any good to just yank them from the surface soil; in order to permanently remove them, you must dig them out from their roots.

Before you start doing this, however, you first need to identify your weeds. Removing these nuisances involves addressing your negative, limiting beliefs, as well as developing more flexible ways of thinking and responding to new dating situations. If you're able to eradicate your weeds (negative thought patterns) before planting any new seeds, you'll become comfortable dating, succeed more often, and greatly increase your chances of having a lasting, romantic relationship.

The Weeds Quiz

Think about the following statements, and answer true or false as you read. Keep a tally of your responses.

1. I'll never find someone as great as _____ (the "one who got away").

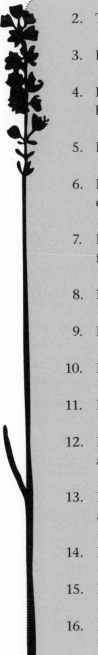

2. There are no good men in this city.

3. I'm too old to find a man and get married.

4. I have to meet someone very soon because my biological clock is ticking.

5. Dating isn't fun.

6. If I were prettier, I wouldn't have any difficulty dating.

7. If I were rich and famous, it would be easier to find someone.

8. Men are intimidated by me.

9. I'm too busy for a relationship.

10. I never meet anyone when I go out.

11. I have children, so I can't date.

12. I can tell in the first five minutes of meeting a guy if I want to date him.

13. Dating shouldn't be work; it should be effortless and feel natural.

14. I attract men, but not the right ones.

15. I feel suffocated in relationships.

16. I can't believe this is the last person I'm going to have sex with.

17. I always find something wrong with the person I'm with.

18. I'd never want to date someone who my close friends didn't approve of.

19. It would be difficult for me to date someone if I couldn't picture him hanging out with my friends.

20. My friends know me well, and if they don't think a guy is a good match for me, I should just move on.

21. I have to admit that it would be hard for me to date someone whom my sibling(s) disliked.

22. It's almost impossible to imagine dating someone who is completely different from the kind of guy my mother wants me to be with.

23. It's almost impossible to imagine dating someone who is completely different from the kind of guy my father wants me to be with.

24. When I meet a new guy I like, my first thought is, *Will my parents like him?*

25. I'll only date my *type*.

26. I'd never date someone like my father.

27. I want to date someone just like my father.

*If you answered **true** 1–9 times:* You have some weeds to pull, but you're almost ready for a new relationship.

*If you answered **true** 10–18 times:* You have some serious weeding to do; your soil will soon be ready but not quite yet.

*If you answered **true** 19–27 times:* You're completely overgrown with weeds. Be sure to give yourself plenty of time to focus on your groundwork before even thinking about gathering new seeds.

Pulling Weeds

As you can see from this quiz, there are all sorts of weeds that can crop up in your romantic life. The first step is to identify all the weeds and see what kinds of limiting beliefs are obstructing new growth in your romance garden. Just that simple discovery is a major step, and you should be proud of yourself for confronting your weeds. Now you might be asking yourself, *Okay, I've started to find my weeds . . . so how do I get rid of them?*

There are several ways to pull weeds, including surface pulling, which makes the negative thoughts disappear for a while, but inevitably they come back. If you realize that a specific belief is limiting you, observe yourself the next time it pops into your mind (or you're behaving in a way that's due to this negative thought). Focus on it as if you were staring at the weed growing in your garden. Realize that you're feeding the weed with more negative thinking. By consciously taking notice of when those thoughts occur and what situations trigger them, you'll be ready to pull the weeds and get rid of them for good.

However, be aware that weeds are pesky: They have roots and can grow back. To pull them out from their roots, you have to be vigilant about spotting your negative thoughts and beliefs. Catch yourself thinking things such as: *He didn't call me back, so he must not like me. No one will ever love me.* If you haven't gathered enough information to determine if that's really true (and it probably isn't), you've identified a weed. If you allow an emotionally abusive guy to stay in your life even though you know that he must go, *he's <u>not</u> the weed. Your thought process that allows him access to your intimacy is the true menace.*

Let's take a look at some of Julie's weeds. One of her old boyfriends cheated on her with his ex, which was devastating for Julie and ended the relationship. In her next relationship, her new boyfriend considered his ex to be "just a friend," and each time they met for a quick coffee, Julie's suspicious, jealous thoughts were triggered. To feel better, she'd read her boyfriend the riot act, demanding that he banish his ex from his life forever. She fed her weeds (the negative, destructive thoughts) all of her energy despite the fact that her boyfriend was being open and had no intention of reuniting with his ex. But Julie couldn't hear his pleas because she was convinced that she was right and was consumed by her very real MFDA symptoms. Eventually, her boyfriend could no longer stand the fact that she didn't trust him or give him any space, and he ended the relationship. It possibly cost her a great love.

Our point is that you can pull a weed, but it will grow back if you don't keep on top of it. And it's not enough to have a moment of recognition; you must constantly be aware if certain weeds are popping up. You have to pull them out or dig them up again and again, and then one day they won't grow back—we promise. Break the mental circuitry, eliminate the MFDA patterns, and your garden will be free of weeds.

Let's go back to Julie's story for a moment. Not all ex-girlfriends are threats just because her last boyfriend cheated with his. But it's also okay to have a pang of jealousy when a new boyfriend says he's going to a movie with an ex because she's having a bad day. Yes, Julie was deceived in the past, but she allowed that negative thought pattern to grow and take root in her garden.

If you've been developing trust (and cultivating the seven factors within yourself), you need to be able to pull weeds before

letting them choke your current and future relationships. Examine your weed (why you're feeling the way you are) *before* saying anything to your guy. In this manner, you're not allowing your limiting thoughts to control you. Remind yourself not to let the weed grow back! If your new man has given you no reason to worry about an ex, then take a breath and pull that weed as many times as necessary.

In order to eradicate weeds completely, you must dispute them. For example, it's simply not true to proclaim: "There are no good men out there!" It also doesn't make sense to believe that because you're a single mother with a four-year-old, *no one* will ever want to date you. None of this is logical thinking based on facts. On the contrary, anything is possible. Negative thoughts only become true when you believe them. You must stop feeding the weed and pull it by changing your mind-set.

Yes, Barry dumped you because he couldn't adjust to how much time you needed to spend with your son, but it doesn't mean that Ben will have a problem with it, because perhaps he also has children and is more understanding. Maybe Jake loves kids but could never have them until now. You don't know because you're not a mind reader (despite your intuitive gifts).

Eradicate your weed, hopefully forever. Remember the following phrase anytime your weeds are strangling you: "Is it possible?" *Is it possible* that it could work out? Yes! Replace limiting beliefs with possibility thinking. Of course the answer is always yes because anything is possible until *you* decide that it's not.

Here's yet another way to get rid of weeds: Go back to the Weeds Quiz you just took, and for each time you answered *true,* think of a sentence to dispute that line of thinking. You don't have to come up with a concrete *false* for each one; just allow yourself to see the alternative viewpoint as a possibility.

For instance, yes, he didn't call you last night even though he said he would, and a weed might make you believe that he was out with another woman. But if you pull the weed before letting those thoughts grow, can you see that there are alternative explanations? Isn't it possible that he's just working late? Isn't it possible that something unforeseen has happened but he'll call you in three days, excited to see you again? Yes! And because it is *possible,* you have confronted your weeds with possibility thinking.

(Pulling weeds will make you a happier person because you won't be living with and dwelling on worst-case scenarios, which not only negatively influence your dating mind-set, but also affect your overall state of mind.)

Let's look at ways to refocus your thinking and pull those weeds:

Weed: "There are no good men in the city."

Possibility: Is it possible that you could meet a nice guy in this city? The answer is yes. Of course it's possible (and highly probable) that you don't know every man in the city, and maybe a wonderful new guy just arrived in town today. It's possible, right?

Weed: "I'll never find someone as good as my ex."

Possibility: Well, he's your ex for a reason, isn't he? Didn't you learn valuable lessons from the experience that can now inform your dating life? Yes, it's possible that you'll find someone as good as or better than your ex!

Weed: "We had a great first date, but now it's a week later and he hasn't called. He hated me and will never call again."

Possibility: Try thinking this instead: *Perhaps he's traveling for work or is very busy and he isn't around this week. I don't really know him or his schedule, so I'll give him the benefit of the doubt and wait until he calls me. If not, I'll move on!*

⬟ Wondering ...

Romantic Love Myths That Keep You Stuck and Unable to Move Forward

Does your dating mind-set make you believe any of the following myths?

- Dating should be easy, smooth, and feel good all the time—it should be effortless.

- I shouldn't need to go out of my way; love will find me, and I'll know it immediately!

- The right person will come along someday, so I don't have to focus on dating.

- Dating at my age is foolish.

- You only find true love once in a lifetime, so what's the point of dating?

- It's hard to put myself out there, and it's been impossible to meet someone new. It's just easier to settle for something familiar, like one of my old boyfriends.

How Will I Know When My Groundwork Is Done?

You'll know when you're ready for dating, love, sex, and a committed relationship when you can honestly say that your dating mind-set can support and encourage the growth of the potential romances you'll soon encounter. You're ready when you've identified and started pulling your weeds. You're ready when you're able to assess potential in men beyond a first impression.

We want you to feel *whole* before entering any new relationship instead of looking for a partner to fill your *holes*. You're truly ready to date when you feel that you can share your life with someone rather than depend on a man to give you a life. You're ready when you're okay *without* someone else in your life, but you'll welcome a great guy when he does show up.

Before we move on to the next stage of the SW Method, we want to stress that if you still have a lot of weeds in your garden, take all the time you need to reread this chapter, go over your quizzes, and do more groundwork. This is an ongoing process.

In the meantime, congratulations on doing (or at least starting) this groundwork! It isn't always easy to prepare new soil, as many people are afraid to look into the dark corners of their lives and, instead, simply let their fear control them.

If you can accept the fact that you'll feel insecure and uncertain at times but continue on the path toward transforming your dating mind-set, then you've become *fearless*—you have the courage to face your fears and go beyond them.

Once you've started pulling weeds and your garden's soil has become fertile, it's time to move on to the next step and find some seeds to plant.

Chapter 7

Stage Three: Looking for Love in All the Right Places

Now that you've started your groundwork and decided what types of seeds you want to gather, it's finally time to jump into the action. This is the stage where you're finally beginning the actual *dating* process. You're now officially ready to get out there and meet some men!

As you begin to date, your Ideal-Man Checklist becomes essential, but remember that it's only meant to guide you and keep you on track. It was designed so that you'll have a constant reminder of what qualities you want in an ideal partner when you're out meeting guys. So be sure to glance at your list from time to time. Some women think they can have a hot guy on the side while waiting for a man with real potential to show up, but we discourage this and want you to stay focused on your intention for dating.

Know that you're the one who's in control because you're looking around and making conscious choices to attract men with certain attributes, while also staying flexible and open to new possibilities.

From this day forward, you're different from the many women who just stand around at a bar, waiting to be picked up, and from those who don't even go out for fear of not being hit on or "chosen." In the SW Method, *you* are doing the choosing. You will learn how to position yourself so that you're communicating in a way that tells men they can and should approach you.

Of course it feels good to be wanted and to have the man you're interested in pick *you* over all of the other women out there. However, there's no competition in the SW Method because you'll learn how to use *mystique* to transform your dating possibilities from nonexistent options to being flooded with exciting opportunities.

Gathering Seeds

Most people try to find their Ideal Man by looking for shared interests. You might hear from a friend that Joe loves to play tennis and since you also love to play, you two are definitely "meant to be." Perhaps you're a musician and he is, too, which seems like a terrific connection. Or you both run your own businesses, so you must have a great deal in common . . . hang on just a sec.

These are just surface traits that you might, in fact, have in common, but it doesn't make a guy the perfect one for you even though he might look good on paper.

We had a client who liked to scuba dive, and he spent most of his weekends at the beach. He finally met a woman who also enjoyed diving, and they began to date. Yes, it was fun at first, but he soon found out that she was aggressive and he was a bit more Zen; he was liberal, she was conservative; he loved kids, she hated them; and so on. Even though they enjoyed many of the same hobbies and had a good time together, it wasn't enough to make them a love match. (By the way, our scuba friend ended up meeting the most non-outdoorsy, shy writer, who only liked to dip her big toe in the kiddie pool! However, she was the type of woman who was up for a challenge and decided to take some scuba lessons when they started dating. They've been married for six years now and have two beautiful sons.)

So remember that sharing the same weekend hobbies doesn't guarantee that you're a match made in heaven. On the other hand . . . sometimes it does! One of our other clients loves to investigate ancient ruins and met a woman on one of his trips. They've never been happier and can't wait to get out their boots for the next dig. They don't just have a love of archaeology in common, but this couple also does a great deal of charity work and they're the kindest people on Earth.

It's fine if you're athletic and want a man who gets out there with you on the track or on the mountainside, but please keep an open mind. In many cases, the person you come to love can learn to share your hobbies—or not, which is okay, too. We know one couple who seldom hangs out together on Saturdays; she loves to go to the farmer's market when he goes hiking. They're confident individuals who encourage each other's diverse interests, and their relationship has flourished. Forget Saturday mornings— they have awesome Saturday nights snuggling at home.

We also want to caution you about believing that there's only one "type" of seed for you. As we discussed earlier, if you've de- cided that he *must* have dark hair and broad shoulders, you're severely limiting yourself. In the same way, if a man shows no in- terest in you because you're not his type (blonde with big boobs), he's limiting his choices. Sure, you might find a guy with the physical build or hair color you find attractive, but what if he lacks compassion or doesn't believe in fidelity? Will you cave in and give him an extra chance just because he's your supposed type? One of our male clients was heartbroken when his Pamela Anderson look-alike "girlfriend" was seeing three extra guys on the side. Imagine!

We know a woman who met the hunk of her dreams, who was bookish, sexy, and smart. However, her dark-haired, green- eyed dreamboat would flirt with other women in her presence and was never on time for anything. He also skipped her birth- day and could never be found to celebrate holidays with her. Yet

she kept giving him pass after pass because he fit the bill of her "perfect type."

Be careful with this physical-type business because the guy who looks like Colin Farrell might be sexy, but the regular-looking man who never lets you down and always goes the extra mile is far sexier in the long run.

Slow Down!

In the process of gathering seeds, we want you to remember that you're just looking for certain qualities that you hope a man will have, but you're not quite sure if he really possesses them. As you begin to date, please don't allow your fantasy life to take over the process. Remember to continue cultivating the seven factors (patience, flexibility, mystique, boundaries, information, emotional availability, and faith) within yourself.

For example, Tim might not be the nicest, most giving person in the world just because he called to say that he enjoyed meeting you for coffee. Women have a way of writing a novel around one simple act and weaving an entire fantasy around an action. Yes, it was nice that Tim called, but what kind of person is he? You don't know at this point. In fact, all you know is that he's polite, hot, and knows how to dial a phone. You'll need to spend more time with him before you can make a rational, informed decision about his character.

We're telling you this because at the seed-gathering stage, it's very easy to want to rush to the next step. Remember that right now you're dealing with sketchy knowledge and superficial traits; you'll need some time to investigate.

The Internet and Online Dating

For the most part in our society, we've moved past the days of relying on friends to set us up on blind dates or hoping to meet someone randomly on the streets of our hometown. Everyone leads extremely busy lives these days, so most singles turn to the Internet to meet others who are also looking for love but don't want to hang out in bars or clubs to find it.

Again and again, we're asked how to navigate the Net successfully and with the least amount of frustration and pain. Because online dating and social-networking sites have become so prevalent in our culture, we're dedicating this chapter to the subject. (We'll talk about additional ways to gather seeds in the next chapter.) In the following pages, we'll teach you how to look for romance on the Web safely and effectively, but first we want to advise you of the dangers lurking online.

We know many women who meet and talk to men via e-mail, instant messaging (IM), or chat rooms. They really think that they've gathered the greatest seed, but then the first meeting in person arrives and it's a total disaster. For example, he looks nothing like his photo—he's older, fatter, and shorter. Or he quickly admits that he's not really a lawyer. These women tell us that they're frustrated and disappointed, and are ready to just give up on dating. However, if you use the Net wisely, we think it can be a really great tool.

Always be aware that there's a fantasy component to the Internet. For instance, you connect with someone online and feel there could be real potential so you invest yourself in IMs, e-mails, and eventually phone calls. Despite all this communication, you won't know if the seed you're gathering is worth it until you meet the person face-to-face and spend time with him. He has to show up in the flesh; otherwise, all you have is a false sense of intimacy and the notion that you're close to someone who's actually a stranger. In fact, until you meet him, you don't truly know him or have a genuine relationship. Someone is just telling you who he is, and you're (temporarily) choosing to believe it.

Keep reminding yourself that meeting someone online is just one way to gather a seed that might prove fruitful . . . or not. If you keep an open mind and approach it with this attitude, then you're on the right track!

With that said, here's our complete guide to using the Internet to find potential seeds, starting with the do's and don'ts of writing your personal profile for an online-dating site.

Creating a Screen Name

Your experience begins by creating a screen name for yourself. If you glance at any online-dating site, you will see there are all sorts of interesting screen names that will serve as your first introduction. We recommend that you pick a name that's significant to you but wouldn't be strange to others. For instance, what does "PanamaJohn" *really* mean? Maybe that's an inside joke between "John" and his friends, but it's confusing. We've also seen men go by "Prince Charming," which is as ridiculous and off-putting as the woman who bills herself as "SexyMama69." Women should *not* have a name that says they're easy to get into bed—*period*. It *will* attract men: The kind who just want to get laid.

Basically, you don't have to put that much thought into your screen name: Just keep it simple. We advise you to use your real name, but if it's not available (if it has been "taken" by another user), add a combination of numbers to the end. Now you're presenting yourself in a truthful, straightforward manner. You don't need to come up with a clever or cool name. We think it's a bit trite to be "DogLover222" or "YogaWoman"—just be "Sally972."

Revealing Your Age

Don't lie about your age—no matter what! It's unfortunate that many men in their mid-40s do so because they decide they want kids later in life or simply desire a relationship with a younger woman. So they go online, and instead of admitting that they're 45 (and counting), they shave off a few years and are suddenly 37 again.

So here's Mr. 46-year-old going after a 29-year-old, and he's not planning on telling her the truth until he meets her and shows off his new Mercedes. Instead of being dishonest, however, it would be better and more effective for that man to reveal his true age and write in his profile that he wants to meet a younger woman.

Just be honest about your age because if you build a potential relationship on deception, it will quickly collapse. For example, we had a client who was 30 and started chatting online with a man she thought was 35. However, when they decided to meet at Starbucks, her 35-year-old date revealed that he was almost 50. He played it off, saying that age meant nothing and that "it's just a number." Well, it *did* mean something to her, and she never spoke to him again.

Please don't think a guy you're interested in won't be upset if you say that you're 40, and later he finds out that you're really 44. He can already see that you look great in your photo—and if you're honest, he'll think that you're someone worth pursuing.

Disclosing Your Height/Weight and Posting Your Photo

First of all, just like being honest about your age, you should also not fudge about your height and weight or post a deceiving photo in your profile. Please don't use your high-school graduation picture or some bikini shot from a 1995 vacation in Cabo when you were 110 pounds.

You need two recent pictures: a clear head shot and a body shot. You shouldn't be standing in the dark or in shadows in either of them. And if you've changed drastically since posting the photos, be sure to update them.

You should also pose alone—not with friends or a cute guy you know. That's not screaming, "Look, guys like me!" Instead, guys checking out your profile will wonder why you're hanging

on some dude and will think it's odd. (Many men post photos of themselves standing next to some slutty-looking girl, thinking it conveys an image of "I'm desirable," yet it's actually a huge turn-off.) In addition, don't wear anything that's too revealing; you shouldn't feel like you need to show off a lot of cleavage or any other private part. You'll only draw guys who want to have sex, not a committed relationship.

Finally, unless you're a photographer, don't take a self-portrait, or you could end up with some horrible or unflattering close-up of your face. Ask a good friend to take some pictures, and then upload the best ones. Yes, you can do great hair and makeup, but don't go overboard so that it looks like you're at the Academy Awards.

Now let's get to the height and weight thing. Many dating sites ask for your specific measurements, but we don't think you have to reveal this information. If you're using recent, good-quality photos of yourself, then your weight and height range will be obvious. When describing your physical build, choose words that feel comfortable and are accurate, such as *fit/athletic* or *curvy*. However, don't leave the body-type field blank, or most men will assume that you have a weight problem.

Writing Your Profile

It's important to consider what you're going to write in your profile, and once again, we want to shout it from the rooftops: *Be honest!* Unfortunately, many people write half-truths, exaggerate their attributes, or compose grandiose stories about themselves. Please don't think that this will help you meet a great guy.

If you're dishonest, then you're really boxing yourself into an impossible corner. Let's say that you do meet an amazing man; however, one of the first things he's going to learn about you is that you're a liar. He'll eventually discover that you weren't a Dallas Cowboys cheerleader or Miss America runner-up who has a record deal at Sony and a modeling contract with Elite. If you're serious about a committed relationship, tell the truth and know that the right man out there will want to meet the real you.

Another mistake is that many people don't write about who they are—instead, they write about who they want to be, but that's a big no-no because that imaginary individual isn't going to show up on the first date! The jig will be up during the initial meeting, so please be aware of that fact and save yourself from a potentially embarrassing situation. The objective of your profile isn't to sound cool, ultra sexy, or to present the fantasy of the perfect woman. Don't say that you own a business when you're thinking of starting one someday, and don't claim that you run marathons if the farthest you've actually gone lately is to the fridge and back.

In your profile, a lot of dating sites will also ask you questions that seem like some sort of pop quiz, such as "Are you adventurous and spontaneous? Are you warm and caring?" We hate these yes-or-no questions because they're usually meaningless. Who's going to respond with: "Frankly, no, I'm not caring at all. I'm a self-absorbed jerk!"?

Be careful when you're reading someone else's profile and see the words *warm, caring,* or *kindhearted.* Those traits can only be revealed over time after you've gotten to know the person. Everyone believes that they're loving and friendly, but the proof will be when those traits are actually exhibited in the real world.

One of our clients shaped his profile in order to find the woman he thought he wanted. He wrote that he loved to hike, and his ideal mate would have fun exploring nature with him. On most weekends, however, he wasn't in the woods; he was in front of the tube watching shows about nature. When we asked him why he didn't start hiking now (and said that he might even meet a woman on the trail), he responded, "I'm waiting to meet the right girl first, and then we can hike together. Unless someone else motivates me, I won't get off the couch." This attitude is a big, big mistake.

Answering Common Dating-Site Questions in the Best Way

In addition to your profile, many dating sites include open-ended inquiries such as, "Tell us about yourself." The problem is that if you write too much, it sounds contrived or you may appear too self-involved. If you go on and on about your cat, Milly, and your involvement in PETA, you might bore the men who are initially interested and they'll wind up thinking you're some crazy cat lady. By the way, you can't really tell these men who you are; they'll have to figure it out after meeting you.

When you're answering these types of questions, the goal is to provide a brief description of yourself. Talk about a few of the things you're interested in while keeping it to one paragraph. Don't write a novel, but don't write four words either. Know that less is more as you compose a simple bio. *Don't* write: "I'm fun, funny, and outgoing"; *do* write: "I'm Jan from Chicago, and I'm a CPA who likes to boat on the weekends. In my spare time, I listen to jazz music and eat pizza. I also love traveling in Europe." Just provide a snapshot of your life.

One word of caution: Don't say anything sexual. We know a woman who, on the advice of a male friend, included this in her personal profile: "And in bed, I'm willing to try anything—I'm adventurous!" Well, she did get tons of hits from interested guys, but they just wanted to have, um, an "adventure" with her.

One dating site poses this statement for members to fill in: "My ideal relationship is. . . ." We believe that this is ridiculous and encourages fantasy. It's far better to depart from the "prince on a white horse" questions. If you have to respond, we suggest that you write this: "Well, let's meet and I'll reveal that to you slowly." Or you can write that your ideal relationship is "a lasting, loving relationship," or "someone I can explore potential with."

Another site asks: "What is your perfect first date?" Once again, this encourages fantasy. So many men and women respond with: "We'll sit on the beach sipping wine and watching the sunset as a violinist plays a few feet away," or "I'll whisk you off to a romantic weekend in Paris." Don't describe your first date as something out of a movie, with the man greeting you with flowers and you both end up passionately kissing at the top of the Empire State Building. Remember that fantasy just encourages more fantasy and unrealistic expectations. Then when you have a simple Starbucks date, it's a major letdown! Simply write that your perfect first date is having a cup of coffee and getting to know the other person.

Another common fill-in statement is: "I am looking for. . . ." The bogus answer is: "a kind, loving person who will be by my side forever." Instead of that, write that you're looking for someone you can explore potential with that will hopefully lead to a loving relationship.

Income

Many sites will ask what your income is, and we really dislike the idea of someone searching for mates based on how much money they make. Just skip that question. You should state what you do for a living, and that will provide people with a good range of your earnings. Don't lie about what you do, or say what you wish (or hope) to be doing someday, because that will only lead to disastrous results.

Remember the *Sex and the City* episode where Miranda pretends to be a hot flight attendant while her date pretends to be a doctor? She's really a lawyer and he works in a sporting goods store. *Ka-boom!* It's over because they lied.

Religion

You should honestly state your religion, or just write that you're spiritual (if that's the case). If you're unwilling to date outside of

your faith, then make that known in your profile so the hot athe-
ist who's intrigued by you won't waste his time writing. This is a
touchy subject and many people have very strong feelings, so it's
best to be clear and honest.

The Laundry List of Traits

Many dating sites want you to wade through a five-page list
of traits and check the ones that best describe you. We find that
this self-reporting isn't accurate. Some sites will also pose questions to determine if you're introverted or extroverted. Remember that a lot people don't answer honestly and instead try to
make themselves sound as good as possible. It's nearly impossible
to accurately list all of your own qualities.

So what if you think you're spontaneous and daring? If a guy
you meet asks you to go white-water rafting next weekend and
you decline, he may think that you're not spontaneous *or* daring.
Does being adventurous mean that you love hot peppers on your
hot dogs or that you jump out of airplanes? Perhaps it means
that you sometimes wear a see-through shirt and black lace bra,
or bungee jump off bridges? We think it's amusing when these
dating sites ask if you're open-minded. Who would ever write
otherwise? "Nope. I'm very closed-minded, obsessive, and I have
low self-esteem. I pretty much hate everyone and think the world
sucks."

Just fill out these parts to the best of your ability, realizing
that when you're reading various men's profiles, these laundry
lists aren't reliable. We like the idea of answering in a lean way.
If they ask you to list 25 traits about yourself, just offer 10. Go
through the list and try to be honest instead of just reporting
what sounds good. Have a few reasons in mind why you believe
you have specific traits.

Many sites also ask this biggie: "What are you looking for in
a man?" One woman we know wrote: "I don't like men who are

bossy." That spoke volumes about her need for control. We tell women to keep this answer brief and state that you're looking for someone who's smart, kind, and compassionate.

Loaded Questions You Should Never Answer

One dating site we checked out asks: "What went wrong in your last relationship?" We don't think you should ever answer a question like this. First of all, many people never figure out exactly what did go wrong. Plus, this is your personal business; we advise you to leave that question blank. You certainly don't want to write something like this: "He cheated on me with my best friend—the pig!" That says you're a victim and maybe you did something that drove your lover to your best friend. It's never a good idea to respond.

Likewise, there are sites that ask supposed "fun, sexy" questions. One even asked: "How many sex partners have you had?" and "Have you ever considered a three-way?" Don't answer anything that seems too intrusive or sexual in nature. You might even reconsider joining a site that places too much emphasis on sex.

Should You Join More Than One Dating Site?

We think it's fine to become a member on a bunch of dating sites because what you're really doing is tossing out a large fishing net. You want to gather as many seeds as possible and not invest too much time in any one place. Decide how many sites you want to use based on how many "hits" you're getting. Start off with one, and if you're receiving considerably fewer e-mails every day, then join an additional site. It's similar to going to various bars in your neighborhood and deciding which attracts the best crowd.

How to Proceed after the Initial Contact

Again, we can't caution you strongly enough not to start an e-romance where you spend weeks e-mailing a guy but not meeting in person. This isn't the way to get to know each other before the big date; rather, you're investing too much emotion into him and may end up creating huge expectations that most likely will prove disappointing.

Our method is to exchange two or three e-mails, and then say, "Do you want to talk on the phone?" If the phone call goes smoothly, then arrange a short coffee meeting to see if you want to go out on a date. Don't talk on the phone more than once. (Remember, you're encouraging a fantasy relationship if Bob shoots you an e-mail every morning and calls each night before you've even met the man face-to-face.) It's easy to think you've fallen for someone when you just talk on the phone. This is because you're falling in love with an ideal that you're most likely creating in your mind.

If you do this again and again with Internet seeds, it will prove exhausting and heartbreaking. Your well will run dry (remember, water is your emotional availability), causing you to want to give up on dating. The same goes for texting this new person a million times a day. Yes, it's exciting to receive a text message from a new man, but it will eventually burn you if you don't like him in person, or vice versa.

Once you've gathered a seed, go meet him. When it comes to gathering seeds, our motto is: *Investigate. Don't invest.*

Should You Date Guys Who Aren't "Geographically Desirable"?

Many women we know don't confine their Internet search to men in their own city or even their own state. They make it clear in their profile that they'll consider men from around the country, if not the world. The reasoning behind this is that your perfect match might not live in Atlanta, so why not allow men from all over the place write to you? Why limit your options? Let's think about one thing: Can you really go to Rome to have a coffee date with a new guy (even though we're sure the coffee would be amazing)?

We've found that people who only look for those who live far away might not be ready for a real relationship. Dating is best done in person; you don't want to put all that distance between you. Plus, the whole long-distance relationship forces you into a number of traps, including spending all of your time on the phone, e-mailing, or texting.

You might not believe it, but you should stick to people in your own town. If you open it up geographically, then be sure to look for guys who are interested in relocating. In addition, check out men in a city that you're willing to move to as a basis for your search. If you meet a great guy in another state and neither of you is willing to move, then what's the point? Don't operate on the fantasy that he'll fall for you so deeply that he'll change his mind and relocate for you.

The majority of long-distance relationships don't work, so we don't advise gathering faraway seeds. If you have a history of out-of-town crushes, is it possible that you don't really want to see someone regularly right now? Or perhaps you desire the grand gesture of someone having to get on an airplane or drive several hours to see you.

Also consider that if you like Marcus and start this long-distance relationship with him, what will you do when you call him on a Friday or Saturday night and he's not home? Will you go crazy thinking he's out with another woman? Distance often creates jealousy and doubts, which fuel MFDA. What will happen when he's supposed to fly in and visit you some weekend but has to cancel at the last minute because of work? To truly explore potential, you need to see each other in person, and feel each

other's energy while gathering information. It's very hard to water that seed from 2,000 miles away, and you can't feel that same kind of energy via text messages or phone calls.

Many men from out of town will contact you to have a brief flirtation. They might not even want a real relationship and perhaps are just looking for strictly online communication or phone sex. They're happy to remain just a picture and voice in your life, and have no intention of *ever* spending money on a plane ticket to see you. You also have to consider that the cute guy from Michigan might really be a guy from New Rochelle who's married with three kids.

If you do explore an out-of-town seed, send a few e-mails and have one phone conversation. At that point say to him, "I'm excited to meet you when you can come to my town." *Boom!* He needs to come to *you*. We're old-fashioned in that manner in the SW Method (more about that later). If this man is truly interested, he'll make travel arrangements; if he won't, there's no point in continuing to correspond with him. You don't need to go through three months of e-mailing (as expectations build up) to finally realize that he's not going to get out his Visa and buy that plane ticket.

A Final Note of Caution

We started this section discussing the dangers of online dating, and it's vital to reiterate how important it is to exercise caution. Remember that while the Net can be a great place to meet men, it can create an illusion of closeness. We have a client who lives in New York but wrote and spoke to a man from Colorado. They couldn't meet after their first few calls because both were bogged down with work, but they made plans to get together over Memorial Day weekend.

They e-mailed each other every single day and called each other often. To our client, it seemed like love—how could it not be when they discussed deep feelings, hopes, and fears with each other? When they finally met—at this point, so much expectation was built up—he seemed different. He was quiet, withdrawn, and didn't discuss much more than the weather and why his ex-wife was such a cheating bitch. In fact, this pair had one awkward steak dinner, and then he flew home the next morning without even telling her he was leaving his hotel. He called from the airport, meekly saying that he was needed at home. She never heard from him again.

Our client was heartbroken at first but then realized that once they met, she wasn't enamored with him either. He seemed to be a completely different person from the one she e-mailed and spoke to so often.

We caution you not to create a fantasy around someone you haven't met in person; this isn't a successful or healthy way to date. When you're typing on a keyboard or hiding behind a phone receiver, it's easy to be a different person. Don't create fantasy after fantasy on the Internet. Always briefly talk to the guy you're interested in, and then meet him in person to find out if you still feel the same way.

In the next chapter, we'll explore additional ways to gather seeds, including going to bars and trying out speed dating, as well as focusing on how your body language helps tell men what you want.

Chapter 8

Stage Three, Continued:
Even _More_ Places to Look for Love

Bars, Restaurants, and Clubs

No matter what you think, you're not too old, boring, lazy, or tired to go out once in a while. We think bars, restaurants, and clubs are definitely good places to meet men. You'll find people who live in your area, have similar lifestyles, and who are probably also interested in meeting someone with relationship potential. Be flexible and open your mind to the possibility that you could meet a man unexpectedly while you're out having fun with friends.

Our first bit of advice is to pick a place that you're comfortable in—that is, the atmosphere fits your age range and lifestyle. For instance, if you're 40, you may not want to look for men at a rowdy college bar unless of course you're a cougar (an older woman who prefers younger men). If you're going to clubs, be aware of what kind of "scene" they attract and even what type of music is played. This information is easy to find in your local paper or online. Don't spend too much time scrutinizing this, though; you're just going out to have a drink with a girlfriend, socialize, and maybe meet someone new. If you don't, at least you had fun, got out of the house, and communicated that you're ready and available!

Remember Your Ideal-Man Checklist

As you begin to date, the checklist you made in Stage One really comes into play now. Remember that your list was designed to help you envision the kind of man you want to attract. Keep it with you to prevent you from falling back into old behaviors; your list should be a supportive reminder of the characteristics you truly desire.

Yes, we agree that while you wait for a man with real potential to show up, it might be tempting to hang out with that funky, good-looking rocker guy who still lives in his van down by the river, but wait . . . does he exhibit the qualities you really want in a serious mate? We know he's mysterious and gives you butterflies, but we're pretty sure that you didn't include these items on your list:

- Must live in a van
- Is financially dependent on his parents
- Has no clear career goals

Don't waste your time and energy on someone who isn't capable of having the kind of relationship you want. We encourage you to stay focused on your objective: dating according to the SW Method in order to meet a really great guy who turns you on in multiple ways. Remember to continually access your internal romance garden (and do your groundwork) to keep yourself on track throughout the process. For instance, when having a fling with the van guy, realize that he's taking up valuable root space and using up essential nutrients in your garden.

Casual hook-ups are problematic because you end up draining the *water* (emotions) from your internal well, rather than conserving and using it down the road when someone with real relationship potential shows up. If you just want to cultivate relationships with random hot guys that bloom quickly and fade after one season (three months is one season in the SW Method), that's your choice, but we encourage you to manage your resources and concentrate on growing something that could bloom for years.

What Should You Wear Out?

The clothes you wear can communicate a message about your intention. We know a woman who walked into a bar wearing one of those supershort shirtdresses with bare legs and stilettos. She was hit on by every guy looking to get laid that night and pretty much ignored by those who were interested in meeting a relationship-minded woman. Does your look say that you want to explore a committed relationship or that you want to spend a night at Motel 6? Use your smile to attract attention—not your sex appeal.

Understand that being sexy is beautiful, but we encourage you to leave something to the imagination and avoid exposing yourself. If you wear a blouse that reveals everything down to your nipples, you might attract the kind of guy who's looking for a one-night stand. If the men you meet are staring at your body and not into your eyes, you may want to rethink how you dress.

Select a few "going out" outfits that are flattering and feminine—not your work clothes! We suggest you avoid pantsuits, conservative office attire, uniforms (of any kind), baggy sweaters, T-shirts with company logos or funny sayings, clogs (or other clunky shoes), or more than one article of clothing that's black or gray.

Keep it simple with a fun top and your favorite jeans. Look for a color that complements you, such as the sweater that everyone says "brings out your gorgeous eyes." A formfitting top is fine, but avoid showing too much cleavage. Don't overdo it on jewelry,

either: Earrings are nice, but don't wear ones that are overwhelming or way too large. Cute sandals or boots can make an outfit unless they're uncomfortable and you're limping around all night. Invest in a good-quality, chic pair of shoes that are feminine, fit well, and have a decent heel. You don't want to be teetering on stilettos, but having even a small lift is more feminine and sexy than shuffling around in flip-flops or Crocs.

And, of course, don't overdo it with your hair and makeup, which could communicate that you're high maintenance. Remember that a little goes a long way. Here's a tip: Guys love lip gloss. It's simple, sexy, and comes in a variety of colors. Choose one that suits your skin tone and brightens your face.

Cultivating Your Mystique

We're revisiting this very important factor because developing mystique can drastically impact your ability to meet men and will ultimately improve your dating success. Let me (Ryan) explain how vital it is: Even though you may not realize it, women have *all* the power in the dating process simply because men can't resist a woman's mystique. When women are in touch with that special *something* that they all possess—the soft, sensual allure of femininity—it's extremely enticing to men. Women who exude mystique stand out in a crowd. It's not just a pretty face that causes a man to do a double take—when women feel comfortable with themselves, their natural grace and sensuality are the most powerful aphrodisiacs.

Women with mystique don't rely on surface beauty for attracting men. They know that their feminine energy is captivating, and they project a sense of mystery and charm. They *feel* desirable, sexy, and confident; and this is clear to every man they encounter. In fact, it's like a magnet! The big difference between this and *oozing sex appeal* is that mystique attracts men on a level that goes beyond physical attraction. It's how a woman communicates her sense of self, her self-esteem, and her personal boundaries (no neediness or clingy behavior here!). Her sexiness comes from conveying: *You'll have to prove yourself* instead of *I'm easy.*

Learning how to tap into your mystique while dating will help you in countless ways. It's easiest to think of it as the *opposite* of desperation: When men see that you're calm, confident, and captivating, they'll want to know more about you. Sometimes it's also the challenge that comes from the nonverbal messages that men pick up from you that compels them to seek you out. For example, if they feel like "She doesn't need me" or "She's happy with or without me," the *air* you exude causes men to enter that "I have to have her in my life" state of mind. Of course, if you're following the SW Method, he won't *have* you at all, and that will just make him want you more.

If you'd like to watch a great example of a woman with mystique, rent the movie *Sabrina* (the classic starring Audrey Hepburn or the remake with Harrison Ford; both are great). Sabrina is the shy and awkward daughter of a chauffeur who has spent his life working for a wealthy man who has two sons. She has been infatuated with David (one of the sons) all of her life, but he hardly notices her. After spending two years in Paris, exploring her interests and developing a strong sense of self, Sabrina returns as an elegant, sophisticated, beautiful woman. Suddenly she finds that she's captured the attention of both sons. Imagine that!

She became *captivating* and *magnetic* without an extreme makeover requiring plastic surgery, a personal trainer, and a fake tan. Everything that made Sabrina attractive *was already inside her.* She just had to learn how to access her mystique and let it shine.

Sometimes when we teach our students how to use their mystique to its full potential, we encounter resistance. Many women believe that changing their dating persona or consciously flirting is manipulative or contrived, but we strongly disagree. Projecting feminine energy isn't dishonest—it's every woman's birthright. In fact, all the ways in which women mask their femininity is what's deceptive and unauthentic.

Women have been trained to de-emphasize their femininity

in the workplace—and that's appropriate in many cases. We certainly don't suggest that you exude sexuality at your next staff meeting! However, resist the urge to bring your work persona out with you on a date. After years of perfecting a serious exterior, don't fool yourself into believing that projecting your feminine energy will make you look weak or dependent. Many women don't realize the power of their mystique and try to impress men with all of the qualities that they've relied on—like most modern women—to achieve success in the business world.

For example, Bianca met Travis at a bookstore. They were both interested in healthy cooking and bumped into each other (literally—he backed into her when he was reaching for a book) in the cookbook aisle. Their first formal date was at an Indian restaurant that they'd both been dying to try for months.

Their conversation was flowing smoothly until Travis asked Bianca if she'd like to have some wine and suggested a sauvignon blanc that he enjoyed. Bianca, who's a wine connoisseur, told him that she didn't really like that one and went on about her immense collection. He tried to get back into the conversation by mentioning a highly rated chardonnay that he'd recently bought on a wine-tasting trip in Napa, but Bianca made sure to mention that she also had that in her collection, as well as the award-winning reserve edition from 2002.

Bianca did what we call *one-upping* and became competitive, having to prove that she was better or smarter than Travis. You may wonder why she'd do that, but she thought she was impressing him. This is fairly common behavior; in fact, many of our male clients have told us stories of women who at first seemed great but quickly revealed that they had "something to prove." While these women are engaging in verbal combat, they're actually forgetting about their mystique completely.

This is no secret, but men are *not* looking to compete with women. Men prefer women who are sensual rather than argumentative. If you're coming off as overly aggressive or competitive on dates, this could indicate that you aren't really open to meeting someone yet. And incidentally, it's very *unattractive* to men.

Rather than verbally communicating your worth and value to men, learn to use your mystique to *show* your power! Luckily for you, women who follow the SW Method convey a natural *air* of mystique because they project confidence and intrigue. They feel empowered to meet better men and make smarter choices. When you follow the SW Method, *you* are in control and can remove the word *desperation* from your vocabulary—forever!

Tips for Accessing Your Mystique

So you've sworn off one-upping men and have watched *Sabrina* three times. Now what? Do you have to go to Paris to find your inner mystique? Of course not! Remember, it's inside you and has been there all along—you've just hidden it. Here are some ways to connect with your feminine energy:

- Take a bubble bath. Treat yourself to scented bath salts or foaming bath oil. Light some candles and soak in your radiant sensuality.

- Wear dresses more often. Yes, you love your favorite skinny jeans, but nothing feels more feminine than wearing a dress that fits you perfectly.

- Put on some sexy nighties. Time to put away the flannels and old T-shirts. Whether or not you have a special guy, wear something lacy to bed.

- Buy yourself fresh-cut flowers—their beauty and fragrance will awaken your feminine energy.

🍃 Have a spa day. Whether alone or with your girl-friends, getting a massage or facial can make you feel pampered and feminine.

🍃 Keep your skin soft and smooth. Apply a fragrant, sweet-smelling lotion and enjoy your own sensual touch (you can even touch yourself *there* if you want to).

What Is Your Body Language Saying?

In the dating world, body language is primarily used as a flirting method where gestures, poses, postures, and facial expressions are intended to convey interest *or* disinterest to others. This may include consciously smiling at someone, making repeated eye contact (or batting your eyes), using specific "come hither" hand movements, lip licking or applying lipstick, body positioning (toward or away from someone), playing with or twirling your hair, putting your shoulders back, and pushing out your chest. Your body language is constantly telling men what you think of them and whether you're interested in what they have to offer. Learning how to consciously send signals to communicate interest is critical for dating success.

The signal should be subtle—exaggerating body language gives the impression that you're overeager or desperate. And sexually overt signals may send a strong message that you desire casual sex, not a relationship.

The biggest problem we've seen for women meeting men at a bar or club is their own conflicting body language—yes, ladies, *you* can often be the problem. Avoid sending mixed messages, and make sure that your body language supports what you're feeling. For example, if you're at a bar and you unconsciously smile at a guy who won't leave you alone, he can't help but think, *Hey, I think she digs me!* On the other hand, you're thinking, *Can't this dude get lost?*

Tune In to Your Body Language

A recent study conducted by the Ludwig Boltzmann Institute in Vienna, Austria, revealed that many women interacting with men at bars and clubs often project body language that's contrary to what they're feeling internally. Researchers found that whether or not the women knew it, most of them exhibited positive body language (such as making eye contact) even when they weren't interested in a guy. Likewise, women displayed more negative cues (such as arm crossing) when they did like someone. "There was hardly any difference in the number of courtship signals [body-language cues] given off by those women who did express an interest and those who didn't," said Professor Karl Grammar, who conducted the study. "And the women who said they were interested in the man gave off more negative signals than those who weren't interested."

We've seen it time and time again: A woman spies a cute guy, looks at him once, and then frowns as she turns her back on him. The original warm smile vanishes into thin air. Even when the guy attempts to make eye contact with her again, she tenses up and looks away. Why? Usually because she doesn't want to appear "easy" or that she's "coming on too strong."

Now let's look at it from the male's point of view. I (Ryan) want to make sure you understand that a guy clearly interprets this to mean that you're not interested. Plus, he sees your timid smile and thinks that you may be smiling at another man or waiting for your boyfriend. He sees an attractive woman and she looks interested for a minute—smiling, looking his way, and trying to establish eye contact—but then she instantly turns away or perhaps even flirts with another guy. He's done—at least with you.

If you're sitting at a bar with your girlfriends, it's even more intimidating for a man to approach all of you. Now he's thinking, *I have to think of some dumb line to impress them or make them*

laugh. Many women unknowingly make the mistake of going out in a pack. Then they stand in a semicircle, getting frustrated because men aren't coming up to them. They don't realize that they're communicating the opposite of what they intended. They're closing themselves off to "outsiders," and guys read this as "I'm out with the girls, so don't approach me."

To Drink or Not to Drink—That Is the Question

First and foremost when it comes to body language, a major no-no is the drunken "I'm looking for some loving" signal. When consuming alcohol, we recommend a two-drink maximum. If you decide to meet men at bars and clubs, remember to control how much you drink. We know that many women can polish off four Cosmos in an evening; however, it's not necessary—you can certainly get a nice buzz from two drinks. You don't want to get drunk, because an intoxicated woman is more likely to make stupid choices and throw good judgment out the window (in addition to the fact that you're making yourself vulnerable to potentially dangerous situations). For instance, we don't want to see you acting wasted in the club and making out with some guy you met ten minutes ago. We can pretty much guarantee that you won't see him again, and he won't think, *Wow, I have to call that cute, drunk girl who was all over me the other night. I think I want to settle down with her!*

Alcoholic drinks are probably the most widely used substance for the alleviation of anxiety. I (Dr. C) want you to be aware that alcohol is also a powerful depressant. Some evidence suggests that consuming alcohol to alleviate anxiety may be counterproductive, as it can lead to a higher or irregular heartbeat and a lowering of blood sugar, which can both add to unpleasant MFDA symptoms.

It's All in the Eyes

At a bar or club, it all comes down to eye contact. Your eyes are your most effective tool for expression because they communicate the most about you—they're even known as "the windows to the soul." Anger or hurt can be masked in the body, but your eyes somehow express the whole truth (and often more than you even want to reveal). This is why eye contact feels so personal and should be used effectively.

When you see a guy at a bar who looks interesting, we suggest using the SW Method's **Three-Looks Technique**, which is basically establishing eye contact with a man three times. The first look is the initial discovery of a guy, the second is the confirmation that he really is as cute as you thought, and the third is a way for you to smile and perhaps play with or flip your hair quickly.

Here's how it actually works: As you're looking around the room, is there anyone who's cute or seems attractive to you at the moment? When you do spot a guy who might be promising, make eye contact with him and then look away. If you liked what you saw during that initial contact, try to get another quick look into his eyes and at his appearance. After looking for a second time and you're becoming more interested, make eye contact for a third time and smile. The third and final glance says, *Hey, you're cute. It's safe to come talk to me.* It doesn't say, *I'm sleeping with you tonight!*

If our Three-Looks Technique seems impossible to do because you're too shy, then it's time to go back and do some groundwork. Shyness is one of the weeds in your garden.

What Signals Are <u>You</u> Sending to Men?

As we've said, most women are generally unaware of the messages they're sending to men. Since these signals are powerful indicators of attraction, knowing what you're physically communicating will help you show interest and send the types of signals that men feel comfortable responding to.

Do You Communicate "Stay Away"?

When you're at a bar, do you naturally cross your arms or square/hunch your shoulders? Do you stiffen your posture or turn away when you see a cute guy? When you're out, are you overly attentive to your girlfriends and find yourself engaging in intense conversation with them? You may be interested in meeting someone, but your body language is clearly saying "Stay away," and men aren't likely to approach you. Women are often surprised to hear that they're doing this—especially when they think they're really open to meeting people.

Women with "Stay away" body language may not be ready for a relationship, or they may be nervous in social situations. As a defense, they're communicating that they don't want to be approached as a way to avoid the dating process.

Do You Communicate "Easy Lay"?

Although this doesn't imply that you actually are an "easy lay," you may be sending signals that suggest otherwise. Do you touch a guy's arm or leg when you're chatting with him? Talking about sex, having lots of physical contact with a person you just met, and getting drunk all communicate: "I'm open for business." You may want to go out, have fun, and meet new people, but all of the bending over and crotch watching won't help you find a satisfying relationship.

Signature behaviors of "easy lay" body language include:

🍃   Looking him up and down

🍃   "Crotch watching"

- Showing lots of cleavage

- Bending over to show off the "junk in your trunk"

- Touching a guy (holding his hand, putting your hand on his thigh, touching his face, backing up into him)

- Drinking beyond our recommended two-drink maximum

Do You Communicate "Come My Way"?

When you're out at a club and you meet a cute guy, do you make eye contact and smile? When you're sitting at a bar are your arms uncrossed? Do you make sure to go out with just one girlfriend when you're hoping to meet someone new? Congratulations!

Your body language communicates "Come my way"—meaning that you're sending clear signals to men that you're available and approachable. This will give you the best chance of meeting someone with the most potential for a serious relationship.

Advanced Techniques

Even a "Come my way" girl can improve her body language by learning an advanced technique called *mirroring*. A great way to communicate that you're attracted to someone is to intentionally emulate the other person's gestures and posture (for instance, leaning forward when he leans forward, smiling when he smiles, or crossing your legs in the same way as his).

It's a fact that when we like people, we mirror their behavior. If the first meeting is going well, this is something that you'd actually do naturally, but you can also intentionally mirror another person's gestures and posture. It may feel weird initially, but the guy you're interested in will think that you're clicking really well.

What Should You Say to Men When You're at a Bar?

Now that you're clear on body language, it's time to focus on verbal communication. Okay, let's say you've made eye contact a few times with a really cute guy you met in a bar, and he saunters over to have a short chat. What should happen next?

The purpose of talking to a man in a club or bar isn't to interrogate him or interview him as if he's the next Supreme Court nominee. Be yourself and act casual—laugh about what's going on around you or bring up something you heard on the news that day. You shouldn't ask him about his life plans or whether or not he wants a house in the burbs and three kids. That's a major turnoff.

If you need to know within five seconds of meeting a guy whether he wants kids and a pool in his backyard, then you have some weeds to pull in your soil. Likewise, if *he* starts to grill you, make a mental note of it because he's suffering from MMDA.

How to Establish a Connection with a Guy

Let's say you met someone interesting, and you'd like to get to know him better. What should you do next? In the best-case scenario, you'll have already sent clear body-language signals that indicate your desire to see him again, and he'll ask for your phone number. If you prefer, it's okay to give him your e-mail address instead of your number. Just say, "The best way to contact me is through e-mail." This is the safest and most effective way to approach dating using the SW Method.

We don't encourage women to ask a guy for his number. We know that as a modern woman you certainly can ask him out and some guys like this initially, but it doesn't set the best precedent for dating when you're using our system. We stress this because if you're hanging out with a new guy and he *doesn't* ask for your number, he's sending a clear signal that he's not interested or that he has a girlfriend. Whatever—it's not a big deal. So he's not your Prince Charming after one night of talking in a bar—move on! Yes, perhaps he enjoyed spending a few moments with you, but he wants it to end there. Thank him for the great conversation and focus on the next moment, whatever that may be: on to the next bar or home to check your online-dating responses.

We've heard many women lament, "But maybe he's too shy to ask for my number." I (Ryan) want you to know that *when a guy likes you, he is never too shy to ask for your phone number. Never!*

If you talk to a guy who may have promise, give him your e-mail address and walk out of the bar instead of flirting with two or three other guys. If you were lucky enough to meet one guy who has real potential, don't waste any more time or try to make him jealous.

One of our clients thought that flirting with multiple guys in front of a man she was interested in made her more desirable to the guy she really liked. But let me (Ryan) tell you how it is: If he sees you flirting with other guys after spending time exchanging contact info, he'll think you're a game player. He probably won't e-mail or call you. Who needs the hassle?

Should You Give an Annoying Guy a Wrong Number?

If you don't like a guy after talking to him for a while, don't give him a fake number. It's a cowardly act, and it's mean to have someone walk away thinking that he has a chance with you . . . until he discovers that he's called the local pet store.

At the same time, a lot of women feel bad when a guy asks for their number but they're not interested in dating him. They don't want to hurt his feelings or be insensitive,

so they give him a fake phone number. However, it's better to be honest, and it stings less for him in the long run if you say, "No, I don't think that's a good idea. It's not feeling like a match for me, but thank you for asking."

Then politely say good-bye and walk away. Be very clear in your body language and you won't have to be a bitch to get him away from you. He'll respect your classy handling of the situation. Although it can feel awkward, it's much better than deliberately deceiving the guy, who may end up calling a wrong number five times and feel burned.

If a man persists because he thinks you're playing hard to get (perhaps you're sending mixed signals to him), walking away is a clear-cut sign that you're *not* interested. Be firm in your stance but polite.

Always be clear about your intentions. If you meet a loser and let him hang all over you or grind on you on the dance floor, then he'll get the wrong idea. If you're not interested in a guy who's a little less offensive, then talk to him for a minute and say, "That was fun. See you later."

Handling Rejection

Picture this: You're sitting at a bar and the night is winding down. You've been talking to this interesting guy, and he hasn't asked for your phone number, but he doesn't go away either. You know that the bar will close soon, and you have the feeling that you'll never see him again. So you might be tempted to say, "Hey, do you want to come to my place and hang out?" Absolutely do not go there! You may also want to say, "Hey, do want to walk over to the coffee shop next door?" *Wrong, wrong, wrong.*

End the night—and don't feel that you need to plan a date or you'll lose the guy.

I (Ryan) can't say it enough times: "If the night is over and he wants to see you again, he'll ask how to contact you if he's truly interested."

Remember, you don't really know this person after a little chitchat. So you spoke, laughed, and spent some time with this cute guy. You had a drink and told a few stories. He still doesn't know you very well, and you don't know him. (That's why he can't come to your house!) If he walks out the door into the universe without writing down your e-mail address, then just chalk it up to an interesting night out—no harm done. At least you're putting yourself out there and are open to the possibilities that could change your romantic life forever. You never know how these things will turn out.

What If He Asks for Your Number?

If a guy you're interested in asks for your number, this is good news, but you need to keep your emotions in check. Calmly reach into your purse and scribble down your name and e-mail address: one address and nothing more. Please don't write down ten different ways for him to contact you because it will look like you're needy and desperate—not to mention a bit ridiculous.

If the night is still young after he gets your info, resist the urge to go out with him somewhere that evening. Like we said, don't go for coffee, and never say, "Well, it's only midnight and I'm starving. Instead of getting dinner next week, why don't we go to Denny's right now?"

Remember, you have time on your side, and you'll see him again. Allow the anticipation to build and intensify before that next encounter. Waiting will turn him on much more than if you just go to the next bar with him and then kiss passionately in the cab. You don't have enough information yet to move this fast, *so slow it down.*

🛑 Wondering . . .

The objective of the SW Method is to put the date back into dating. In other words, you want him to date you formally, so make him arrange the next meeting. You don't need coffee, breakfast, or a hook-up *now*. You need to give him your e-mail address and get the hell out of there!

It's a myth to think that you're missing out on wonderful moments if you don't stay out with him until dawn. Those whirlwind romances always end up burning out in a month—and you know it! Even if he suggests that you go to another club with him that night, you should say, "Scott, I'm having so much fun, but I need to go home. Talk to you soon." Or you could also say, "I can't abandon my girlfriends, but I had a great night with you. Why don't you e-mail me this week, and we'll set something up?" He has your e-mail address (or number), and it's his turn to take the next step.

Again, you're forcing him to date you formally, and you're not allowing it to be casual. And remember that in this stage, you're here to *gather seeds,* which you did by talking, flirting, and giving him an e-mail address or phone number. Your job is done for the night! So at the end of the evening, always have an "out" (somewhere to be) and force yourself to go. We promise that the guy will actually be intrigued by your mystique and will probably call you sooner than you even expected because you followed the SW Method.

By the way, there's no need to hug him or give him a quick kiss before leaving the club or bar. You're following a formal dating system and intimacy comes much later, so give him your best smile and head for the door. If he leans in for a hug or kiss, step away and say, "Not yet." Physical contact occurs at a later stage in the SW Method (which we'll discuss soon), so for now use this phrase. It's very effective, too, because it's slightly seductive but firm.

What Happens If He Doesn't Contact You?

If he doesn't call, don't go on a hunger strike or OD on Oreos. You have only one way to act here: *Let it go.* You don't know if he was as great as he seemed—come on! He may have been married or even a sex addict—you just don't know. We say this because we know women who make all kinds of excuses when they give out their contact info and never hear from a guy again. They think, *Maybe he lost that piece of paper? Maybe I should call him? I remember he said he worked at—*

Stop! And if he doesn't get in touch with you, don't return to that same bar ten more times hoping that you'll run into him. He'll find you if that's his choice—unless you're currently in the Witness Protection Program. Believe us when we say that there has never been a case of a man writing down a woman's number on a cocktail napkin, losing it, and then *her* calling him, only to have it lead to a 40th wedding anniversary and 12 children together. (*As if!* If this *has* happened to you, drop us a line and we'll apologize!)

Please listen to your buddy Ryan here because I assure you that if a guy gets a phone number and he's excited about the girl, he's not losing that number even if he's in hurricane conditions. That little number isn't going anywhere. However, if he doesn't reach out and contact you, don't personalize it. Maybe he has a girlfriend or had some second thoughts about dating. (Despite what you may be thinking, he probably wasn't attacked by a great white that chomped off his back pocket where he'd slipped the paper that had your number on it—that damn shark!)

Please don't build this up emotionally or feel heartbroken. He was investigating you just as you were checking him out. You spent a little bit of time together over the course of one evening, and that's not cause to shed a tear or call ten girlfriends to mull over the "what-ifs." Anyway, why would you want a guy who disappointed you even before the first date?

The Creepy Guy

You're in a bar and the creepiest guy wearing a Members Only jacket from the '80s gloms onto you and won't go away. This is an excellent time to practice saying no and setting boundaries. To get rid of the creepy guy, you've got to stand your ground and say something like this: "It was nice meeting you, but I'm going to go talk to my friends now." Don't worry about coming off as cold or arrogant because all you're doing is being firm and direct. This is essential: Leave no opening or question about your interest. Say what you need to in a polite, conversational tone and then physically move away from him.

Let's say you wander over to your friends and Creepy Guy follows you. You've probably experienced this before or at least watched it happen to one of your friends. When this occurs, turn around to him and say, "Thank you, again, but I need to talk privately with my friends." Then turn your entire body away from him, putting your back to him. If he touches your shoulder, face him and calmly say, "Please don't touch me again. I'm not interested, thank you." He should get the hint.

If you're out for the night with your trusted "wing woman," you can create a special "Get me out of this" signal. When you give the sign, your girlfriend can approach the two of you and say, "I have to steal her away."

Don't be worried that you're hurting his feelings. You don't know him or owe him anything except one polite refusal. Believe us, he's a big boy and he can handle it.

Out of the Club and on the Streets

If you're truly ready to date, you don't have to be at a bar or club to gather seeds. Notice your everyday environment: Make eye contact and smile at others when you're walking down the street, shopping in a neighborhood store, or working out at the gym. And even if you're feeling lonely or would rather be somewhere else, don't go through each day at your job appearing unapproachable because you're scowling and gazing at the floor. When you look that way, the cute guy who works in the next department might be checking you out, but he'll think, *Nah, she's not interested.*

Don't let your weeds get in the way. We have a client who honestly believes that if her celeb-knockoff hairstyle doesn't look perfect, she better keep her head down and not smile at guys. She projects the air of "Don't look at me because I'm insecure." She's not open to new people, and the same goes for women who walk around in a fog, staring into the distance or texting friends. Their body language also says, *Don't approach me.*

So let's say that you get all dolled up, go out there with gusto, smile, make eye contact, and then find yourself home two hours later watching reruns of *Oprah*. Well, bravo for you, because you got out there and maybe even had fun. When you took more time than usual to do your hair before heading to the post office (the *new* singles bar, people say), maybe you didn't gather a seed that day, but you practiced carrying yourself easily and confidently (tapping into your mystique) and maybe someone noticed you who hasn't even revealed himself just yet. You'll never know if you spend all of your time at home watching TV.

Here's another tip: Stop walking around with your cell phone surgically attached to your head! That makes you very unapproachable. You're much more likely to meet someone if you're not engrossed in conversation or pretending to text someone. Let's say you're at a UPS Store, and a cute guy is standing in line next to you. Pull your weeds and don't let MFDA cause you to doubt yourself or stare at the floor (or pull out your cell phone). If you behave

in this way, you're making sure that nothing will happen—when something could. Which way do you want it to go?

Religious and Cultural Beliefs

There are many people who identify strongly with cultural or religious beliefs. To them, it's important that their partner also share their views. Attending events at places of worship can be an excellent way to find a partner who shares your values.

For example, Jackie spent years looking for love at work, through friends, at business school, and even on the Internet. Her mother kept telling her that she'd find her ideal mate at church, but Jackie wasn't interested and thought that her mom was just being old-fashioned. After a dating drought, however, she finally gave in and went to a church social. She was pleasantly surprised to find men who were in complete alignment with her beliefs and exactly what she wanted in a mate. She eventually met Rod, who fit her Ideal-Man Checklist to a T. They're getting married soon—yes, at the church where they met. (By the way, Jackie's mom can't stop gloating!)

Matchmakers

There are many professional matchmakers who charge several thousands of dollars for their services but promise that you'll meet eligible, often rich professionals who will sweep you off your feet. We're sure there are some success stories out there. However, taking this route to meeting eligible men is not only expensive, but it's also based on you telling a stranger (the matchmaker) information about yourself and your dating goals, and then hoping that they're able to set you up with someone who has similar interests and hobbies. In other words, you're paying someone a lot of money to link you up with men based on all the superficial qualities we've already discussed.

Please don't think that making a large financial commitment will guarantee your chances of meeting a great match. These dating systems are only as good as the people who run them. You should always inquire about a matchmaker's credentials. We know of one who's also a dog trainer on the side. *Huh?*

Ask to review a matchmaker's bio and résumé. What is his or her background? It's okay to ask questions before you write a check. Any professional matchmaker who finds this insulting or won't give you clear answers should be avoided.

Speed Dating

Speed dating is a recent phenomenon that has swept across most major cities. Basically, you pay a fee and show up at an event where singles are given approximately five to seven minutes to introduce themselves, blurt out some personal information, and then move on to the next person. At the end of the event, you can choose the guys you'd like to meet again and speak to in a longer forum. Many of our clients have tried this approach, and we don't want to rule it out as a way of meeting new people, but we've heard that many men are just there for a one-night hook-up. In addition, a lot women walk away from an evening of speed dating without any guys "choosing" them, which makes them feel insecure and unworthy.

If you want to try speed dating, we suggest that you be open to the experience but have no expectations of how the event will unfold. If you feel that you've connected with a guy but he doesn't feel the same, it's not really a rejection. If you create a fantasy around your ten minutes with someone, then you'll be opening yourself up for a world of hurt. Spend some time tending your soil instead.

The Friend Setup

Friends can be a good way to meet men, as they know what you might have in common with one of their guy friends and can hopefully match up similar lifestyles or values. But all of this can be iffy because friends often unintentionally set each other up on dating disasters. If a friend insists on setting you up, don't plan a blind date. Instead, arrange a small get-together with a few people at that friend's house, or maybe four or five of you can go out for dinner. Say to your friends, "You know I'm single and that I'm looking around. If you know a cute guy I should meet, let's all go out one night."

Even though this is a first meeting, it's not a date—it may or may not have potential. Resist feeling pressure to like this guy because your friends are invested. Please don't believe everything your friend tells you about the man. In fact, don't ask for too much information or you'll invest too much emotional energy well in advance of discovering whether there's a spark between you. This also creates false intimacy, as if you already know this man simply because you have a friend in common. And just because your friend thinks this guy is a great catch, it doesn't automatically mean that he's a person you should date. It's just a link—no more, no less.

You may wonder if it's okay to ask to see a photo of this guy before you agree to meet him, and we think it is. Why go into a situation where you have absolutely no idea what someone looks like? It's not uncommon or rude to say, "Can you send me a photo of Alex? I want to put a face together with the name." You're just doing a little exploratory work. If the man isn't attractive to you, you might not want to meet him. You're *flexible,* though— right? You just want to see him.

If you can't plan a dinner party or some other group event, you can agree to meet this man for a quick 15-minute coffee introduction just as you would with a guy you met through the Internet. By the way, you don't have to bring a girlfriend with you.

We see women do this all the time, but we feel that it's better to go into the situation alone, have a quick drink, and then decide if you want to proceed with a formal date.

If it doesn't work out, simply thank your friend for trying and say, "Alex is a really nice guy, but I'm not feeling a connection. It was great to get a chance to meet him, though." Everyone will understand.

Saying No

When you put yourself out there in the modern dating environment, you'll inevitably meet men who are also trying to meet someone with relationship potential. Let's say that you've met a nice guy who's serious about wanting to date, but for some reason, you're just not feeling it. You want to be polite and not hurt this guy's feelings, but you really don't want to go out with him. What are some ways to turn him down?

Situation: Your running buddy suddenly asks you out. You like jogging with him, but that's it. You thought he was just your guy friend, but all of a sudden, he seems to have other ideas.

Solution: Say something like this: "I really enjoy running with you and we have a lot of fun, but I'm not interested in going out. I don't think we have that type of chemistry, but I'm flattered and thanks for asking."

You're actually helping the guy by being clear about your intentions. It's better for him to know that you're not interested and have a few awkward moments than

you being forced to find a new jogging trail because you're not being clear and he's persisting. This also works with a co-worker who asks you out but you're not interested. Just say, "We get along great at work, but I'm not interested in going out."

If you don't want to date someone, you don't have to lie and say that you have a boyfriend or come up with some lame excuse such as, "I'd love to go out, but I'm leaving for Africa for the next six months." Your life is none of this guy's business; don't feel like you have to cushion the blow because it's okay to turn someone down.

So just say no—and mean it.

A Final Word on Meeting Men

Don't get depressed if at first you can't find a guy that you'd be interested in dating. Each day is a fresh start, meaning that you can step into the world and experience something new and exciting at any moment. So put yourself out there because you don't know what's in store for you.

If you were bummed because you had no luck meeting anyone at happy hour on Monday, you might be elated on Tuesday when you bump into that new guy, Tony, at your favorite lunch place.

Be aware of the men around you at all times, and make yourself approachable and nonintimidating. If you jog while listening to music and wearing huge sunglasses, you won't meet anyone. So take off the iPod one morning, make eye contact, smile, and see what happens. You might send out a vibe that says, *Hey, I want to talk.*

If you place limitations on yourself—"I don't go to clubs" or "I don't have time to join online-dating sites"—you're severely hampering your chances of meeting someone. If you decide not to go to your friend's dinner party, you might be missing out. How will you know unless you put yourself out there?

These men, the seeds that you've been gathering, may have amazing potential, and now it's time to start planting them to see if they'll grow. You'll be planting more than one seed in your garden, so get ready for your first dates!

Chapter 9

Stage Four: First Dates

Congratulations! You've done your groundwork (your soil is looking good!), you've gathered some seeds, and now you're ready to find out if they'll take root in your romance garden. You've come a *long* way to get here, but remember to continue cultivating the seven factors within you. Before the big date, you need to do a bit more *information gathering,* which in SW-speak is the "pre-date," a quick meeting with a man that will last 15 to 30 minutes.

This initial get-together gives you a chance to see the guy you like *in the light of day* so that you can determine if you want to go on a *real* first date without all the pressure. The purpose of this short pre-date is to decide if he's worth pursuing, without spending too much of your time. A quick coffee or tea is perfect! Your objective is to investigate (not invest) whether or not you two have any chemistry. Just because this guy seemed like your ideal man on the Internet or was charming in a bar doesn't mean that there will be sparks between you; therefore, you're meeting on neutral turf before jumping into a traditional date that could ultimately be a waste of time and energy for both of you.

We know that your fantasy might involve a romantic dinner at the best restaurant in town, followed by dancing, and then a midnight walk along the shore for the perfect first kiss. We must remind you, however, that you don't *really* know this new person yet and can't be sure if you want to invest yourself in a true SW-style of date with this guy. That's why Stage Four kicks off with a short and sweet meeting.

This brief engagement isn't a true date, so you shouldn't mentally treat it that way. Don't buy a new outfit or book a last-minute hair appointment to get Reese Witherspoon bangs because you're having coffee with a new guy. Too much preparation will encourage you to place importance on what's basically just a chance to see if he's truly someone you're interested in . . . he may not be. So don't give in and build up the fantasy with what-if scenarios of what *could* or *should* happen on a successful first meeting. And don't spend the week before exchanging e-mails and texts, which just increases your chances of a major letdown.

The goal is to briefly meet and chat—in a public place, which is safer, too. We can't stress this enough: Don't let a man pick you up at your home, because at this point you don't know if you want this guy knowing where you live!

Planning the First Date

If the short meeting goes well, indicate to him that he can now officially *call and ask you on a real date.* This is a formal date, not "hanging at his crib" with takeout and TiVo. A formal date requires *planning,* and whether that entails dinner at a fun restaurant or a daytime stroll through the park followed by cocktails, it's not casual and that's the whole point!

An SW Method date involves a *plan;* it's *not* a promise to call you Saturday so you can sit around and make out on his couch. That's letting him date you casually—a big no-no! Remember, you're dating with purpose and intent.

Let's clarify something else: A date is *not* him saying that he's going out with some co-workers on Friday night, so you should meet him at Red's Bar around 9. That's not a formal date, and if a guy suggests anything like that, you should say no. We know this may be tough because you want to see him and an impromptu date sounds better than no date at all—and it may seem wonderfully spontaneous and even sexy, but it's not. It's actually thoughtless; if he truly wants to be with you, he can plan a formal date.

Perhaps the great guy you had a cup of coffee with on Tuesday calls on Saturday morning and wants to do something that night. If he asks you on a spur-of-the-moment date, simply say, "No, I'm sorry, Roman. When I didn't hear from you earlier in the week, I assumed we weren't getting together and made other plans. If you want to see me next weekend, call me before Wednesday and maybe we can set something up."

Wow! If he wants to see you, he knows that he has to get organized and make plans. You'll stand out in his mind as a woman with *mystique* and appeal! In the SW Method, the timeline for accepting a date is *no fewer than three days in advance* of the scheduled day or evening. Take your time and make him wait. Let me (Ryan) tell you what's going on in the guy's mind: This will turn him on and get him excited about you. He'll think you're very intriguing and if he doesn't, he probably just wanted to get in your pants and didn't want to work too hard for it.

In the SW Method, you shouldn't talk to a guy every single night in between the pre-date and the first formal date. Limit it to one quick call to make plans. If it's necessary (that is, if an unforeseen time change has come up), an additional call before the date is okay to confirm things. This means that after the coffee pre-date, don't stay up until three in the morning talking to him about your future hopes and dreams. It builds too many expectations, which can actually ruin the upcoming date and destroy any long-term potential.

Now that the first date is approaching, you can finally get excited about putting on your good jeans and "foofing" up your hair for the big day. However, don't involve your parents and all of your friends during your preparation. All that you're doing is going out with a guy who may be great (or not), and it will definitely take many more dates to determine if the relationship has potential.

The Actual Date

What makes a good formal first date? It's one that lets you spend intimate time together in a comfortable setting. Beware, however, because some men might plan *too much* for the first date. We've heard stories from women who've been asked to get on a plane and fly to Vegas for a romantic weekend and stay in a luxurious suite. At this point, you don't know each other well enough for that, and if you accept, he may infer that you're desperate or easy. As I've (Ryan) said all along, when women are too available, men consider them less valuable. But if you say no, it will challenge your guy. And men like challenges—trust me.

Julie made the mistake of going on many short-notice "hang out" sessions, as well as some "big whopper" dates. She knew that they weren't real dates, but she'd defend her actions, saying, "He had play-off tickets to see the Yankees! He had third-row seats at a U2 concert and wanted to take me! There was this bullfight in Spain!" There's no rush because those bulls will still be there next time, and you may have to risk missing a concert or two to ensure that you develop your relationship according to the SW Method.

Our main point is not to be tricked (by your MFDA) into thinking, *It's now or never. If I don't accept, he'll ask some other girl.* Pull those weeds! The kind of date he plans will reveal a lot about his personality. Is he the kind of guy who wants to go hiking, or would he rather check out an art exhibit? This is only the beginning—simply a way to gather more information about whether or not you want to continue seeing him. Now let's get into the nitty-gritty of the first date.

Conversation During the First Date

You're sitting at a nice bistro and start thinking, *Wait, am I a police detective, or what?* Resist the urge to start interrogating your date—it isn't fun or romantic for anyone. You probably don't work for the FBI, so don't act like it!

A former student of ours actually brought a typed list of questions with her (something that she'd written in high school!) and pulled them out of her Gucci purse on a date, to the horror of the guy sipping red wine across the table. The purpose of your first date isn't to extract everything you can from the guy—including his résumé and his hopes and dreams—and then determine if his future includes you (the woman whom he barely knows). Instead, what you want to do is have a fun conversation about seemingly *light* topics as a way of exploring the ins and outs of each other. You want to see how you *feel* when you're with him. You're not there to learn everything about him. It's enough to find out if he makes you think or laugh—or both.

You might want to talk about your job and personal interests, but don't ask if he wants children in the next five years. You might discuss the fact that he wants to open a business, but don't ask about how much money he plans to make or how much he has now. Don't inquire if he owns his home or rents it. Even if he tells you everything, those are just pieces of information that may or may not be indicative of who he is on the inside.

We know it's not always women who ask too much. There are many men who also go off on weird first-date conversations. Julie told us about a guy who went on about how his ex-wife cheated on him, and therefore, he wanted to make sure up front that Julie really wanted a committed relationship . . . yeah, that date was a lot of fun.

On another date, Julie met Geoffrey, a guy who needed to know her political affiliation because he swore that he'd never date a Democrat. This isn't good first-date conversation; you don't want to make the other person feel that the "wrong" answer could get him ejected from the corner table and sent back to his car. If he asks an off-the-wall question, you can easily sidestep it, smile, and say, "Interesting question—I've gotta think about that one a bit and get back to you."

Ways to Gather Information on a First Date

His responses to your comments: Does he say anything insightful? Is he funny, witty, or clever? Is he comfortable and at ease? His responses will give you some valuable information about him, but keep in mind that like a carefully constructed profile on an online-dating site, many men have "rehearsed" answers and comments about career, future plans, kids, and so forth.

Your listening skills: *Focused listening* is characterized by intense concentration on the person who's speaking. When someone is really interested in every word you say and is eager to empathize and connect with you, he or she is truly listening. The impression you can get from your date's words and shifts of energy are communicated and received through multiple senses. When listening to the pace of his delivery, breathing, and inflection (soft or hard edged, tentative or tense), you can gather even more information about him.

What kind of listener is he? Is he really hearing what you have to say, or is it just superficial listening? Is he focusing on you and really paying attention? Are *you* willing to suspend judgment, be quiet, and listen to the content of his words as well as nuances of his expression, voice, and energy? Are you listening deeply to his *unspoken* wants and desires? Or are you just listening for what you want to hear?

Information he provides without being questioned: Take note of the topics he brings up on his own (or what he doesn't bring up). Does he mention that he's excited about his brother visiting from Colorado? Does it seem like he's dreading Thanksgiving dinner with his parents? What topics does he explore with *you?*

The questions he asks: This is a great indication of the details about you and your life that are important to him. Does he ask about your workout schedule? Your family? Your career? Your sex life? Take note of what he wants to know about you, and ask yourself why that information would be important to him. We had a client whose first date centered on her business activities too much. It turned out this guy wanted help with his career. *Next!*

Don't be afraid of silences on a first date. When there's a pause in the conversation, many women try to fill in the blank space with mindless chatter; however, you should hold back and let him speak first because it's a good way to see if he can keep up his end of the conversation. You should also avoid simple yes-and-no answers in response to his questions. If your date is asking about interesting things in your life, it's not time to act like you're giving a deposition. Offer a few witty details about your life, because a one-word response is a real conversation killer. Don't make him pull info out of you—that's an exhausting task.

Let's say he asks, "Do you like your job?" If you say no and then stop, you're making him work too hard to get to know you. Elaborate a bit. For example, "It's a good opportunity for me, but

it's really competitive. One day I hope to start my own small company." Follow that by lobbing one back to him, asking, "Now what about you? Did you always want to be a history teacher? I loved learning about the Civil War back when I was in school."

In addition, don't just reply with generic responses (or what you think he wants to hear), because you're trying to get to know each other. If he asks why you chose to go to the local college, don't just say that it's because they have a great business school and then look blankly back at him. Maybe you could say that it's a top-notch program, plus they offer a great semester abroad: "I spent a wonderful year in Italy, actually. Venice was amazing except for the day when I was on the water and . . ."

Always stick to safe topics that won't allow the conversation to veer into intimate (or embarrassing) areas that could cause the evening to hit the skids. Don't ask him why his marriage failed (even if you're curious) or what he thinks about the Catholic Church these days. Don't explore his theories on *Roe v. Wade* or whether or not he supports capital punishment.

A few safe topics for a first date include: work, hobbies, interests, friends, living situations, or pets. This isn't the time to ask what he thinks of the Clintons!

If he goes off on a weird topic, just smile and listen. Julie couldn't believe it when the guy she was with on a first date in a fancy restaurant broke out and did a *Three Stooges* routine. He cracked himself up, and even though she thought it was inappropriate, she laughed (through the pain) and then quickly changed the subject to cool vacation spots . . . as soon as his Moe impression was over.

The 12 Commandments of a First Date

1. Be a good listener. Maintain eye contact when he's speaking and focus on what he says, as well as how he says it.

2. Look attractive, but don't look like you're trying too hard. Don't overdo your makeup or show up in a sequined ball gown. Also remember that work clothes are *not* date clothes! Think flattering, feminine, and fun.

3. Never plan a pre-date for a Friday or Saturday night because it communicates that you're way too available. Does it mean that you should lie and say you're busy (but then stay home alone watching the episodes of *Days of Our Lives* you recorded)? *No way!* Make plans for fun-filled weekends, and leave your weeknights for pre-dates.

4. Avoid talking about the following on a first date: exes (yours or his), children, the time you had a threesome, having sex with each other, if he's seeing other people, if he's ever cheated on a girl-friend, the relationship with Mother (yours or his), your therapist, your debt (or even your net worth), your DUI, and so on.

5. Stick to the two-drink rule. *We mean it.* And if you're a lightweight who gets wild and crazy after a few Zimas, don't even think about a second cocktail!

6. Don't reach for your wallet. He asked you out, so he should pay (including the tip). We know this is old-fashioned, but it's also very modern. If he becomes your boyfriend, there will be plenty of opportunities for you to pay for him.

7. Always have an excuse to leave at the end of the date—even if it's going great and you want the night to continue. It prevents you from staying too long and moving too fast.

8. Don't fall into the "love at first sight" trap. If love develops over time, it will be apparent to both of you. For now, keep planting many seeds. Don't fixate on one person even if it feels like he's the One.

9. Don't be too romantic on the first date; romance comes later when you know what you've got. Just have a good time and enjoy his company.

10. Be observant and pay attention to any red flags. Does he yell at the busboy? Does he flirt with your server? Is he constantly checking his BlackBerry while you're sitting there? Always be open to seeing both his positive *and* negative qualities.

11. Remember your body language. Communicate openness and interest in what your date is saying (if you're feeling that way) without any "I'm sleeping with you tonight" vibes or indications. Mirror his behavior if you're digging him.

12. Flirt with him if you find him attractive, but don't kiss (or even hug him) on the first date.

How to Tell If He's into You

Many women spend a short period of time with a guy and think he's the greatest, and then they also assume that the feeling is mutual. Before you fall into the "I felt it so it must be real" trap, learn how to tell if he's developing genuine feelings for you, too.

The "Is He Really into You?" Checklist

- Does he seem excited about your date? If he wants to impress you, he won't leave lots of important details to chance. Does it look like he spent time picking out his clothes, or does it seem like he grabbed a wrinkled shirt from the hamper and ran out of the house? Did he pick a restaurant with a cool atmosphere?

- Did he plan in advance, or think of somewhere to take you on the fly? Did he arrive on time?

- Is he trying to make a good impression? Is he acting like a gentleman? Does he open doors for you? Does he think of your comfort (ask where you'd prefer to sit at the table)? Is he polite (to you and others)?

- Does he ramble on about himself, or does he ask you questions? What is he interested in learning about you? Does he *listen* when you talk?

- What is his body language telling you? Men display preening behaviors when they flirt, such as straightening their jacket or shirt; touching their hair; placing their thumbs in their belt and (subconsciously) pointing toward the genital area; sitting with their legs slightly opened and relaxed; or pointing their feet in the direction of the woman whom they find attractive. He may come back from the bathroom with his hair freshly groomed or slicked with a bit of water. That guy is into you.

The "Are You Really into Him?" Checklist

After your first date, think about the following questions:

- Were you excited to see him, or were you just going on the date because you really didn't have anything better to do on Thursday night?

- Does anything immediately stand out about him? What did you learn about him on this first date? Here are some examples of information you might have gathered:

  — *He is a kind person (he was polite to the employees at the restaurant).*

  — *He's generous (he tipped the server well).*

  — *He's flexible and obviously comfortable with the unknown or unexpected (he reacted really well when the drinks took a long time and when they messed up his order).*

  — *He has good manners (he didn't use vulgar language or touch his cell phone on the date).*

  — *He doesn't have a bad temper or anger issues (he hardly reacted when the bartender didn't greet you two right away; and when that guy accidentally bumped into him, he laughed).*

Dealing with Bombshells on the First Date

It happens time and time again on a first date: You gathered a seed that seems promising, the pre-date was great, and while you're enjoying a glass of wine, he suddenly drops a bomb. How should you handle unexpected or shocking information?

For example, Julie met Stan, a divorced guy in his late 30s who was handsome, funny, sweet, and witty. Over a glass of Bordeaux at a lovely French bistro on their first date, they seemed to be getting along really well; Julie was flirting, and laughing at his stories. However, as they were eating their mixed-green salads, Stan casually said, "Julie, this is one of the best dates I've been on in ages, and I definitely want to see you again. By the way, I might not have mentioned this—and it's really not a big deal—but I'm not actually divorced yet. I'm separated, and we're getting divorced soon. She never understood me."

Ka-boom! The bomb goes off.

If a "bomb" goes off on one of your first dates, pay attention and think about the fallout. It's absolutely fine to decide that this seed isn't worth exploring anymore.

Separated Men

By the way, should you date a man who's separated? We think you should ditch him—stat. We don't think that anyone is ready to date until the ink is dry on their divorce papers. And if a man says he's divorced but he's really separated, he's lying to you. He's misrepresenting himself, and this is significant. What else is he hiding or fudging about in his life? Tell him to call you when the divorce is final!

Don't become the girl who helps him decide if he really *wants* to leave his wife or not. And absolutely don't let yourself be the fun sex partner he cheats on his wife with before going back to her and the kids. If he seems promising, you can say something like this: "Mark, I think you're a nice guy. Please call me again after you're divorced. Thanks and good-bye."

Men who are separated often hate to be alone, so they immediately join a dating site but know that most women won't want to chat with them unless they claim to be divorced. Again, until he's actually divorced, he is still *married*. Look at it this way: In *his* internal romance garden, there's a deeply rooted flower that he's cultivated and nurtured—*his wife*. He doesn't have enough resources available to give you what you need and deserve.

We strongly encourage you to avoid letting yourself be *the other woman*—basically, a wildflower that doesn't need much attention and something he may decide to clear out like a weed after it blooms. That's a role we never want you to play.

Ask the guy if he has a legal separation agreement. Does he still live in the same house with his wife? You have the right to ask those questions if you really think there could be potential. Remind yourself that this man (at least for right now) is *not* available.

After one date, Rob told Julie: "I'm separated, but we're getting divorced soon. Things were never right between us, but I still stick around for my son. Although I live in the basement of our house, I never have sex with my wife . . . I mean my ex."

Having an affair—which is what you'd be starting with him—isn't going to help anyone. The SW Method states that you *don't date married men, don't have sex with married men, and don't have affairs with married men. Period.*

You're Just Not Feeling It

If the first date doesn't seem to be going well, what should you do? We think it's rude to say that you're going to the bathroom and then skip out of the restaurant. Imagine the poor guy who's sitting at the table waiting and waiting . . . until he finally figures it all out. Now that's sort of sad. It's better to get through the meal, say no to dessert, and then say, "Thank you for dinner. It's been nice getting to know you. Have a nice evening."

Only in situations where the guy is overbearing, too physical, or downright rude is it appropriate to interrupt the date and leave. You can say something like this: "I don't think we have a connection, and I'm going to go now. Thank you and good-bye." Be polite but firm!

The best thing to do in most other cases is say, "Thanks for dinner. Have a good night." If he wants to call, you may have to add: "I'm not feeling a spark. You're attractive and interesting, but I'm just not feeling it." You're not rejecting or insulting him; instead, you're gently saying that you aren't a match. Shake his hand and go on your way.

Getting a Little Action

We'll talk more about intimacy in the next chapter, but here's the way we approach it in SW Land: At the end of the first date—even if it was *great*—you'll say that you had a nice time, shake his hand, and then walk to your car. Just shake his hand! (We're repeating it so that you didn't think it was a typo.)

Do not passionately kiss him, embrace him as if he just returned from war, and certainly don't sleep with him that night, even if it all seems so sexy and enticing. For now, stay with a handshake—it can even be a warm two-handed one to emphasize your interest. But if the guy tries to zoom in for the big kiss or hug, take a slight step back, extend your hand, and shake. Dodge the kiss and say sweetly, "Not yet." If he's confused, politely say, "I don't kiss or hug on a first date, but I'd be open to seeing you again." Then get in your car and go home—alone!

This tells him that it's not time yet, but intimacy is still on the table. The phrase *not yet* is an exciting challenge for a man. You've left your date with lots of interesting questions to mull over. He'll drive home thinking about you and when "yet" will be for him. Let me (Ryan) assure you that a guy who's into you

will totally respect this and won't be able to get you out of his mind.

If he seems annoyed by the handshake and never calls again, then this is information about his true intentions. Our point is to make him want you more. As you get to know each other, the anticipation of becoming intimate will only grow and the payoff will be much more rewarding. Our motto is: *Waiting is the new foreplay.* (We promise that we'll talk about this in detail in the next chapter and even show you how to pace physical interaction with the guy you're dating. Hey, don't skip ahead—we know what you're thinking!)

Many women fear that guys won't put in the time or get to know them if they don't immediately jump in bed and show them their best moves. *This is a myth!* We can't count all of our clients who've said they couldn't believe that a man just stopped calling after two weeks of great sex following the second date . . . wait—did they ever actually go on a date?

Once again, let me (Ryan) stress that a man will almost never get excited about the woman he meets at a bar and has sex with that night. He digs the sex, of course, but he's not taking this person seriously. She's easy, in a guy's mind. Our client Alberto concurs and told us, "If she sleeps with me right away, I assume that she does this all the time with many other guys. I'm definitely not considering anything long term with a person like this." Like most men, he likes the challenge of a woman who makes him wait.

Beyond the First Date

Several situations can crop up after the first date, making it important to not become attached to someone too soon. For example, Julie had a great time with Matt but then never heard from him again. They went to a fun fondue restaurant and dipped bread into gooey cheese and traded info about their jobs and hobbies. Julie even told him about her exciting business trip the next day to New York. Matt promised that he'd call her in a few days to get together. He said, "Julie, when do you get back? I think you're great, and I really want to see you again." And then—*nothing!*

Julie couldn't understand what went wrong because his signals were so positive, and now her MFDA was going into overdrive: *Maybe it was something I said . . . my thighs really did look fat in that skirt . . . maybe he was abducted by aliens . . . maybe he has a girlfriend and suddenly feels bad about cheating on her . . . maybe he likes me too much and is afraid of real love—nah! Maybe he's sleeping with ten other chicks. . . .*

Please don't play back the first-date conversation a zillion times—*don't feed the weed!* (You didn't blow it when you burped after the soup course.) There are many things that could be going on, so you definitely shouldn't blame yourself or feel rejected. Stop thinking this way right now. Please!

You may wonder, *Why did he say he'd call me again if he really wasn't going to?* Unfortunately, some men feel that they have to end each date by saying "I'll call you" even if they have absolutely no intention of doing so. This type of guy is usually a people pleaser and wants to end each date on a positive note.

Picture this: You just came home from a terrific first date, and it was so much fun that you have this crazy impulse to call him even though it's midnight. It's just being polite to want to thank him once more for the nice steak and garlic mashed potatoes . . . right?

Don't do it! If this guy also felt sparks between you, he'll initiate the next conversation because he won't want to let you go. He knows how to get in touch with you, and you need to wait for him to make the next move. Even Miss Manners would approve of this plan, so don't start with the idea that you're not being polite by not reaching out. Follow our guidelines and don't cave in to MFDA.

What to Do If He Calls after the Date

Let's say a first date went really well and he calls you that night or a few days later. Once he reaches out (which we refer to as *taking his turn*), you can employ our "Two-Day Callback Guideline." You may think we're encouraging you to play games, but that's not the case. In the SW Method, you're actually learning to properly *take your turn*. Waiting a couple days before returning his call not only allows the anticipation to build, but it also makes it clear that you have a formal process and aren't willing to rush into anything.

The objective of dating is to enjoy this back-and-forth *lobbing* of communication. Who knows what will happen when you "volley" the ball back into his court? However, his ability to take turns at the pace *you* set is very important in formal dating. If he sends a text, don't reply right away. Enjoy your turn, let the excitement build, and wait a day or so before writing: "Thanks, I had a great time, too."

Since you haven't put too much focus on this guy and have been clear with your signals up to this point, he'll know if you're interested in another date, so let him call and formally ask you out again. He'll learn that you expect to be treated in a certain way and that you don't date casually. If he's the guy for you, he'll love this.

So when he calls, follow our "Two-Call Cycle." Phone calls are meant to be brief, friendly, and playful, but in the beginning, their main purpose is to set up the initial dates. If he calls too soon after your first date, you can let it go to voice mail. Remember to enjoy your turn and don't call him right back. Wait two days and then do so because this completes the cycle (he called and you returned it). However, if he does wait a couple of days after your date before calling, you should answer. (If you miss his call, wait until later in the day to return it; and if you get *his* voice mail, leave a short message—without any jokes or insights— simply saying, "Hey, it's Julie. Give me a call back. Thanks.")

For example, let's say you went on a date with a great guy on Saturday. He texts you on Sunday, saying that he enjoyed the date. On Monday, you reply to his text with a brief yet considerate message. If he calls on Wednesday, he should be asking you on another formal date if he wants to see you over the weekend. If he doesn't ask you out, that's okay, but if he calls on Thursday to make plans for Friday night, you're not free. Make him work a bit to date you formally. And remember that if he doesn't call you by Wednesday, start making your own fun plans with friends so you can enjoy the weekend.

Chapter 10

Stage Five: Exploring Relationship Potential

Let's say your first date on Friday night went great, and now it's Monday and you're back to your routine. In addition to your usual work tasks, your day is filled with thoughts about the guy you're interested in: *Will he call? Is this the One? What should I do next?*

Well, you may be surprised to hear this, but to answer your last question, *you should do nothing.* Wait a minute—you're a modern woman who goes after what she wants . . . you don't have to wait around for a man to decide if he likes you. If you want to call him and thank him for a great night, then you should.

You can, but please don't. (You knew we were going to say this, right?)

Instead, practice the SW Method *because* you're a smart woman who's willing to go the distance to see if it's right for both of you. Remember to rely on your mystique—which will speak to him more effectively than calling or texting him. If he likes you, he'll call to see what's going on with you. We ask that you don't *initiate* any calls, texts, or e-mails; simply follow the "taking turns" process we discussed in the previous chapter.

It has to come from him first, because you want *him* to indicate interest. If he reaches out and wants to see you again, he's clearly communicating his desire. This is why you have to let him ask *you* out on a date again. Remember, no hanging out is allowed because you're following the SW Method, setting the pace and the stages for him. He'll take your lead *if* you're leading. If this makes you nervous, I (Ryan) want to remind you that men want to be put in this role because it feels more like a challenge. If you've been honest and clear in your communication, he'll know what to do! And he'll know that you expect the dating process to remain formal.

If he doesn't reach out, make sure to manage your MFDA weeds and prevent yourself from doing something that would derail the relationship's potential. If you're worried that he may not call, please don't call him out of insecurity—he'll smell an air of desperation from miles away. Instead, focus on cultivating the seven factors in yourself and see about pulling those weeds.

Many of our clients complain about feeling rejected when a guy doesn't call them back. If he doesn't ask for a second date—or reach out in *any* way for that matter—the simple fact is that he's not interested in pursuing you. *That shouldn't hurt your feelings.* If it does, MFDA is present. Perhaps you just weren't a good match for him. Don't forget that *you* won't feel a spark with all the guys you meet either. Both of you need to *feel it* for a match to be made; remember, "It takes two to tango."

If you want to go on another date, but he hasn't called you, let it go. If he's not communicating with you, you have to be willing to move on. Sure, you could force the issue and reach out to him. You may feel better in the moment because you'll know where you stand, but this isn't an ideal dating approach. You may succeed in getting a second date, but you can't overcome the fact that he's not feeling a connection in the way that you are. "Sparks" signify the potential of a relationship, and they're either present or not. Who needs a second date with someone who's just going through the motions?

Don't get depressed if he loses interest, because *your happiness doesn't depend on a guy;* besides, you've been gathering and planting many other seeds at the same time, right? At this point, you should be exploring relationship potential with other men, too. So you have far more interesting seeds to spend time with than one who has lackluster feelings for you.

Moving along the SW Method

Now let's say he *does* call by Wednesday to ask for a weekend date. If he says, "Hey, let's hang out this weekend," stop for a second and remember that he's not following your system. You may need to gently guide him along and say, "I'd be open to going out on another *date* with you."

However, maybe this new guy *does* call with a plan. He wants to take you to the zoo on Saturday followed by a romantic hot-dog lunch in the park. Fantastic! Okay, this may not be your idea of a perfect date, but this shows forethought on his part; he did some *planning* and wants to do something fun with you.

Even if going to the zoo really isn't your thing, resist the urge to nix his plans and suggest something totally different (such as going to an art gallery and then lunch at a tapas bar). Instead of telling him that you have something else in mind, just say, "I'm not sure that zoos are my thing, but I'd still like to go on a date with you. Could we do something different?" If you think he's interesting and want to see what happens, go out with him again (but let him figure out a new plan).

The SW Dating Cycle

We're now entering the next phase of our class. This is where we teach you the secrets of our 12-Date, 3-Month Dating Cycle that will guide you from the first date to a committed relationship.

Although the second, third, and fourth dates (and beyond) really aren't that much different from the first date, your objective throughout remains the same: Have fun and keep gathering information.

While you're dating formally in the next few weeks, set the pace with body-language signals, and let him know that he has to call within three days of when he wants to see you. Why? You're busy—you have a life, and there are other men you might want to date! You'll have to manage this schedule and teach him the process without explaining too much. He'll learn what the various phases are by the messages you send him. We don't think you need to tell him that you're following the SW Method. You're already giving him a peek by making him date you in this formal way.

Here's how your dating plan works: You'll go on one date each week for three months—that is, you're not going to see each other every day. You're not even spending the weekends together. In addition, you shouldn't call each other every night of the week following that romantic dinner you had. Allow yourself these 12 formal dates, because you don't officially know if a committed, long-term relationship is viable yet.

Why not see him every weekend night if you like him? This is a question we're asked time and again, and the answer is simple: It's because *you don't really know if you like him.* You only like what you see *so far,* but is this who he really is? *Time* will tell, and there's still farther to go—11 more dates, in fact, if he's to become your boyfriend (or whatever you call someone you're in a committed relationship with).

We know it feels "hot" now, but will that heat be a fire that you can sustain into the future? Let's look at the standard way of dating where you have one or two good first dates and then hang out every single day. Just because you're spending all of your free time with someone for six weeks in a row, it doesn't necessarily mean that you've grown closer. You've probably just spent a lot of time making out in front of his new flat-screen TV.

The key to the SW Method is to cultivate this potential throughout the entire process before determining whether you really like him. Got it? No funny stuff, because pacing yourself is the objective!

Logging several hours with someone in a short period of time may give you the false impression that you're closer than you really are as a couple—because you're not a couple yet. As you know, remember to investigate before you invest. And whatever you do, don't *overwater* the young seed and cause it to drown. You want to enjoy feeling the anticipation of what's to come, patiently allowing sexual energy to build before fully acting on it and going from first kiss to intercourse. This is why seeing each other once a week makes perfect sense. Remember that you're not building your life around this man, and you're also still going out on dates with other men.

During these three months, don't talk to each other for three hours every night on the phone. You should chat once or twice during the week to make plans and briefly engage. Continue to *take turns* throughout the process of calling, e-mailing, or texting. We do think that you should increase your time for these activities each month, but be sure to manage your resources (and tend to your soil).

Pace yourself, and don't IM him all day long, either. (We see your fingers already on that keyboard!)

Seeing Other People

Let's say that you're four weeks into the system with a guy and he says, "I really like you, and it bothers me that you're talking to other men. I don't want you to see other guys."

You should respond with something like this:

"Ron, it's more comfortable for me to use a formal process so that I can explore potential connections with a few different guys to see if I have chemistry with any of them. You and I are still getting to know each other; I assume that you're also talking to other people and are going out on dates to see if you're more attracted to some-one else. Ultimately, if we have the best connection, we'll get together and have a great relationship. Did I mention that I'm not having sex with other guys? In fact, I'm not having sex with anyone until I'm in a committed rela-tionship. I want to see who's the best match for me. If you have feelings for me, I'd like to continue dating so we can get to know each other better and see how our potential grows."

As you enter the second or third month of dating, it may be enticing to just hang out at his house and watch a movie, but you shouldn't do it. *You still need to have formal dates.* You don't have to dine at a four-star restaurant every Saturday night, but each date should be planned and should demonstrate thoughtfulness. You can have drinks on the steps of a museum while the sun is setting, or go for a hike and have a picnic lunch. Encourage him to be creative! Talk about what you enjoy, but allow him to do the planning. Resist the urge to take over the whole thing.

Men love a challenge and you're putting him in a position where he must think of ways to impress you (and show you a good time). While slowing the process down and setting the pace (so to speak), you're also finding out invaluable information about him as he plans these dates.

How to Date More Than One Guy at a Time

You can schedule dates during the week and weekends, or even have a lunch *and* dinner date on the same day. Why not? You did your hair and put on a cute outfit, so make the most of it! Remember that you aren't spending all day with the person; you're simply going out for a few hours.

Many of our clients find it challenging to see more than one person at a time because they say it's too difficult to keep track of all of the communication and scheduled dates. To solve this problem, we've developed a tool called the *Calen-Dater* to help you manage what's growing in your romance garden and what's going on with each of the men you've been dating over a period of time.

Here's an example from Julie's Calen-Dater. We've included a weekly view so you can see how to keep track of your numerous communications and dates. There's also a summary to help you clearly evaluate each relationship's potential.

You can download your free Calen-Dater at **www.StopWon deringBook.com.** To get the most benefit from your Calen-Dater, you need to use it regularly, noting every call, text message, or e-mail you receive (and from whom). This will also enable you to maintain the two-call cycle with ease. On the right side of the Calen-Dater, there are two headings: Weeds That Came Up This Week and MFDA Symptoms. Keep track of your feelings and emotions as you interact with men, and note specific thoughts that come up. In this way, you'll recognize when MFDA symptoms are overwhelming you. If this occurs, you need to do more groundwork.

The Calen-Dater

Monday
Dave: e-mail
Leon: phone call
Max: e-mail
Bret: e-mail

Tuesday
Leon: pre-date
Bret: e-mail

Wednesday
Dave: phone call
Bret: e-mail, text

Thursday
Leon: phone call, text
Bret: phone call

Friday
Dave: 2nd date
Leon: e-mail, phone call
Max: phone call

Saturday
Leon: text
Bret: phone call
Max: 3rd date

Sunday
Bret: text

Weeds That Came Up This Week

- I'll never find someone as good as my ex-boyfriend.

- I have to meet someone very soon because my clock is ticking.

- Dating is *not* fun.

- If I were prettier, it would be easier to find someone.

MFDA Symptoms

Mental:
- I can't stop replaying phone conversations and dates in my mind

Emotional:
- I feel depressed because Bret didn't ask me out this week

Behavioral:
- I'm calling Bret and Leon too many times

Physical:
- I noticed that my palms were sweaty during date with Dave

- I had trouble sleeping after breaking it off with Leon

Calen-Dater Weekly Summary

Name	E-mails	Phone Calls	Text Messages	Date Number	Gathering Information	Potential (1-5)
Dave	1	1	0	2nd date	• A little shy • Polite (opens doors for me) • Likes tennis • Enjoys his work • Doesn't call me that much • Nice to other people	4
Leon	1	3	2	Pre-date	• Lots of contact in the first week! • Not as much fun in person • Seems a little depressed • Made a sexist comment	1
Max	1	1	0	3rd date	• Very successful • Really busy with his career • Always late to dates • Fun to hang out with • Drinks a little too much	3
Bret	3	2	2	None	• Slow to plan a first date • Discloses a lot of personal information • Is very "into" me • Talks about the future • Wants to have phone sex	4

Evaluating Potential

Monitoring your dates (and even being more aware of weeds that pop up) will become much easier if you consistently use the Calen-Dater. As you record information about the men you date (such as how many times someone calls or even noting observations about a person's traits) you'll be better able to explore the potential of your relationship. Based on the information Julie gathered over time, she could use the Calen-Dater to evaluate the potential in each of her relationships. The last column in the weekly summary is labeled *Potential,* which rates your overall feelings for a guy you're dating. (The scale is from 1 to 5; a 5 is the highest rating, signifying a high amount of potential and chemistry, and a 1 is the lowest.) There are no correct answers because it's based on your impressions, and this may change each week. This is why it's important to continually update your Calen-Dater so that you can look back over a few weeks to review the information you've gathered for each guy (or help recall certain experiences with them).

As you can see from Julie's entries, she went on two dates with Dave and gave him a 4, which means she thinks their relationship has a lot of potential. She listed many of his positive qualities that she observed on their dates. On the other hand, Leon scored a 1 because he was too eager and less fun in person than in his phone calls. Julie also lowered his score because of a sexist comment he made during their pre-date. Max scored a 3 because he seems like a great guy, but his romantic relationships take a backseat to his career, and Julie thought that he drank too much.

Finally, Julie gave Bret a 4, but he didn't deserve it. She soon realized that he was one of those online-dating creeps who has no intention of ever meeting in person anyone he chats with— she even found out that he has a wife and kids. Julie went back and crossed out the 4 on her Calen-Dater and put in a 0!

Let's Talk about Sex

Casually hooking up is a terrible way to explore relationship potential because, in most cases, it derails something more serious before it even gets off the ground. In the SW Method, sexual intercourse signals commitment. (If you don't want to have sex at all, that's your prerogative, but our techniques still apply and can help you determine whether or not this person shares your values.)

We don't judge anyone's sexual history; however, if you're following the SW Method, you shouldn't be jumping into bed with the guys you're dating—that is, dating many men simultaneously shouldn't be considered "slutty." Remember that our method is about *capturing the excitement of anticipation* over a long period of time as you get to know someone and grow closer, eventually becoming sexually intimate if you choose. The objective is to allow the anticipation to intensify while not making impulsive or rash decisions.

If you follow our system, we promise that you'll have a much more fulfilling sexual experience with the man you ultimately choose, and *the wait will have been worth it.* Our clients tell us again and again that they're so happy they'd waited. But how do you accomplish this task in the modern dating environment when most people practically go from first kiss to intercourse?

You must learn to effectively and honestly communicate your *boundaries.* We know you may be concerned that the guy you're feeling deep feelings for won't want to wait because he might think you don't like sex or that you're frigid. We want you to stop worrying this instant.

For starters, if a guy simply doesn't understand why you won't let him rip off your jeans, he probably isn't the guy for you. However, there *is* an easy way to communicate how things will progress sexually, and we want you to try this conversation template with him:

"I really like you and think there's potential for us, but I don't want to move too fast. In the past, I've done it the other way and jumped blindly into passion and it didn't work out for me in the long run. So I want us to take our time and explore potential together, and we'll see where it goes."

One of the principles of the SW Method is: *Waiting Is the New Foreplay.* To execute this *slowed-down, paced* sexual expression and experience how amazing intimacy can be (by building anticipation), we provide you with an innovative system to follow. Stick with us for a moment and we'll explain.

When you were young, your experiences with kissing a boy and really making out with someone were incredibly exciting, but unfortunately, many adults are missing that joy and intensity in their sex lives. Things these days are rushed, but guess what? Those thrilling moments can be recaptured! With our system, you'll be able to manage the slowly developing sexual relationship that many men want to consummate sooner rather than later. We offer you guidelines that you'll find comfortable, familiar, and extremely enjoyable.

Waiting _Is_ the New Foreplay

Foreplay describes all *the good stuff* that leads up to the main event, including touching, hugging, caressing, kissing . . . you know the rest. Your goal is to slow down the process so that you both really enjoy and relish each stage of physical contact. It is the *waiting* to get to each new step that builds the anticipation. So as you explore sexual chemistry throughout your 12-Date, 3-Month Dating Cycle, remember that these are *guidelines,* not *rules.*

Here's how it works: We recommend adding one new sexual progression each week. We call these *moves*—just like when someone "puts on the moves." Some people prefer to try more than one move in a given week of dating, but in the SW Method, we believe that it's best to go one step at a time—from the initial handshake to kisses, eventually to "feeling you up," rounding second base, and finally, coming on "home."

Whatever your preference is for initiating *your* moves, we're *flexible* and offer this only as a guideline. Ultimately, it's your choice; do only what you feel comfortable doing (and when)—you're a big girl now. Our system simply helps you pace yourself and enjoy intimacy without being focused on an end result. It will be fun, sexy, and exciting—we promise!

How to Handle a Guy Who's Pushy

He thinks the idea of slowing down is nice, but he's pushing to get "there" much quicker. For you, simply maintain your boundaries with mystique and playfulness. Let him know that *it* will happen soon if things keep progressing.

Let me (Ryan) explain the male's viewpoint: Most guys remember the days when a girl would stop his hands from going down her pants. Trust me—if you do this, he'll want you even more. Remember, if he can't wait and wants to stop seeing you because of it, don't feel bad. This is valuable information about him. If he wants to sleep with women who give it up easily, he's not the guy for you. Don't let your MFDA weeds grow! If the guy truly likes you, he'll wait until you're ready. Of course it can be hot to have sex right away, but in the morning that guy is throwing your number away. But if you give him a hug and say "Not *yet*," he's intrigued. You're the one who's worth the wait—and the one he eventually wants to bring home to Mom. This move will turn him on.

If the guy just wants to get laid, good luck to him, and good riddance!

Here You Go!

All physical contact should be a conscious exploration of the full spectrum of your chemistry together. As you know, at the end of the first date, you should shake hands. Touching in addition to eye contact is very powerful body language for communicating interest in a second date. It can also signal (with a colder, firm, businesslike manner) that you're not interested but appreciate the first date and have enjoyed meeting him. You can make this handshake more meaningful if your other hand also touches and holds *his* hands as you say good-bye. This tells him to call you. Remember, you shouldn't hug or kiss him on the first date, and if he tries, gently step away and say "Not yet" with coy mystique.

On the second date, you can give him a warm and sensual (but not too much grinding or leg humping, please!) good-night hug. Hugging perfectly paces the developing sexual energy as your bodies lightly press up against each other. Date #3 ends with a closed-mouth kiss on the lips that is soft, sweet, but doesn't linger. This body language conveys that things are progressing, and the day will soon come when you'll both "get more."

Finally, at Date #4, go ahead and try *full-lip* sensual kissing—sucking and biting lips is arousing, and although this signals the beginning of making out, try not to go too far. Your tongues may graze one another as your lips lock, lingering and wanting so badly to open your mouth and give in to the impulse . . . *don't yet!* It will drive both of you wild—which is so much fun!

Second-month dating starts with open-mouthed kissing. This kiss is important because we believe a kiss holds the secret to sexual chemistry. If your kissing goes well, this often indicates sexual compatibility; if not, this may signal a lack of connection. This kiss signals that you're really getting to know one another more intimately now. You may also touch his face, or he may caress your face and neck as he kisses you. Enjoy making out with your bodies pressed up against each other, but no ass-grabs yet—try to stay on the couch. It's too early to move to the bedroom.

The following week brings Date #6, or the halfway point, and now it's time for some *over-the-clothes* groping. "Dry humping" now comes into play, which occurs either in the bedroom or on the couch—grabbing his crotch, him touching your breasts, but not under the garments yet. Contain his hands when they go too far and try to get under your shirt or down your pants, and gently place his hands on the outside of your clothes. No matter how much you want to go further, remember to *pace the passion*.

Tell him "Not yet" and whisper how much you desire him. Talk sexually if you want to, but keep it playful, with hints and promises of more to come. This means that you may have to send him home with a "hard-on," which will make him want you more during next week's date.

Date #7 is time to let him "feel you up." *Yes!* Guide his hands under your shirt if he doesn't make a move. And when you reach Date #8—which is in the second month, by the way—it permits shirts off, skin to skin, and making out without any hands underneath pants and panties.

Date #9 begins in Month #3, and with it comes the full package: touching, hugging, kissing, shirts off, and—yes, that's right—*hands in pants*. At this point, he'll want you so much that he may even try to convince you that it's "time," but "not yet." Soon!

Before moving to oral sex, you may want to try mutual masturbation on Date #10. This is unique because it encourages what many people consider to be a very sexy act: watching each other touch and caress yourselves. I (Ryan) assure you that men love to watch, and although he'll want to do more, this is a major turn-on. The challenge is to contain your sexual energy and not seek gratification through intercourse. This can be a wonderfully bonding and intimate experience. You may find this incredibly exciting, or you may choose to skip this step—it's entirely up to you.

Date #11 encourages oral sex (if you're comfortable). Exploring each other with your mouths is very intimate and an amazing turn-on for the majority of women. Finally, you've reached Date #12, Month #3! It's time for intercourse. As you know, sex communicates a committed relationship with this profoundly intimate experience. If needed, a conversation can occur at this point to ensure that you're both truly committed to this budding relationship.

Here is a chart to help you remember how to pace the moves:

The Moves

First Month (Dates 1–4)	• Handshake • Hug • Closed-mouth kisses • Making out (sensual kissing)
Second Month (Dates 5–8)	• Making out, open-mouthed kissing, no groping • Making out, groping over the clothes • Making out, under the shirt groping • "Feeling you up" • Making out, shirts off
Third Month (Dates 9–12)	• Making out with groping, stroking • Mutual masturbation • Oral sex • Intercourse

If You Have Something to Tell Him Sexually

As a responsible adult, you have to tell potential sexual partners if you have herpes, HIV, genital warts, or anything else that's sexually transmittable. It's your moral duty to tell him, and his to tell you—but when should you do so?

Some men might be understanding if you disclose that you have an STD, but there will also be those who will no longer wish to date you. If this keeps happening, you might want to investigate different dating methods. For example, there are online-dating sites created specifically for singles who have herpes. Please don't be discouraged, as there are many people out there who are in the same situation as you.

But when should you tell someone, and how? We think that the fourth date is the time to bring it up. There's a comfort level at this point, but you're not invested emotionally. You've only kissed and have done a little bit of groping, but you haven't had sex (oral or otherwise). Find the appropriate time, and tell him honestly. You can't take away his right to know something that's medically significant. Yes, it's difficult to do so, but you must tell him. Simply say, "There's something I want to tell you . . ." and let it out.

Know that you're doing the right thing and that you should feel good about yourself. Don't be apologetic or feel like you're ruining a budding relationship. This guy might have something that he wants to tell you, too. More clients than we can count have had these same issues and found that after the disclosure to potential partners, many have said, "I appreciate that you told me. I'm comfortable with it, and I have something I want to tell you, too."

The Other Shoe Drops

Picture this: The guy who has shown potential has waited until Date #4 to say, "Did I ever mention that I have two kids?" Julie was once dating a guy who knew she wanted children, but it took him two months before he divulged the fact that he'd had a vasectomy two years ago, after his last girlfriend got pregnant and had an abortion.

During the dating process, you might encounter a "bomb" and receive new information that dramatically changes your perspective. Don't react impulsively and freak out. What you need to do is take a moment and think about whether or not you want to continue dating this person. Take your time to consider it.

Let's say that he keeps ordering diet colas and never has a glass of wine or a beer at dinner. Then on Date #5, he casually says, "I need to tell you something. I go to AA and I've been sober for two years." You love wine, so this may not work out. You have to seriously consider if you're well matched. These are the choices you must make for yourself.

You're not obligated to give him an answer on the spot. Just say, "Thank you for telling me. Wow, that's a pretty big deal." Then move on to another topic and think about it later. Even if you know your answer, say, "I need some time to think about this." If you decide that it's a deal breaker, don't go home and lament that another one bit the dust. You're not in love with this person yet. *Move on!*

How to Break It Off

Let's say you're on Date #5. By this time, you know this person a little better and realize you're not interested in going out again. What should you do to avoid hurt feelings? Since he's not your boyfriend, it's not a *breakup;* we call this a dating *breakoff.*

When you want to move on, don't avoid his calls. Be up front, honest, and respectful about ending the process. Use kind language and say, "I have something to tell you that's not easy to say, but I must say it anyway. I want to break this off with you."

One note before telling him this news: Don't make a premature decision. Whatever your reasons, check your weeds and MFDA symptoms to ensure that you're not avoiding the dating process. You don't want to make a mistake based on a rash decision and dismiss potential before you *really* know. Give it a chance to grow—a seed that you don't like as much as the others may have a way of shining later on. We've seen this happen time and time again.

The Ex Files

From the beginning, don't open the ex files. What are you really going to gain by learning everything about the failure of your guy's former relationships? What someone tells you about an ex is never objectively true because you can't really figure out what happened without both sides of the story. It's just *his* point of view. Besides, what are you going to do with this information? And what guy will say, "I really was a jerk . . ."? He wants to make a good impression on you.

If he wants to know about your past relationships, you don't have to explain anything because it's not helpful to the process at this point. You can say something like this: "I'd prefer not to talk about old relationships. Maybe we can go back to this topic when we know each other better."

Why do you want to dig through someone else's dirt? Talk about these things once you've reached a legitimate level of intimacy in a committed relationship.

 Wondering...

After three months of dating, you've reached the point where you're certain that you want to explore potential on a much deeper level. Well, we're happy to announce that you've arrived at a pivotal SW milestone. You're ready to consider commitment.

Chapter 11

Stage Six: Entering a Committed Relationship

If you've been following the SW Method, gathering information over a three-month period, the fantasy of *who he might be* has been slowly replaced by the reality of *who he is*.

You're Ready to Commit When You've Stopped Wondering . . .

1. . . . *if he's the One.* Is this guy special? Do you really feel that he's a great match for you? Are you comfortable committing to the possibility of a long-term connection?

2. . . . *if there's someone better around the corner.* Are you still hopeful that someone smarter, more handsome, or more successful will come along? Do you deserve better?

3. . . . *if you can trust him.* Do you have any doubts about his integrity? Is some of the information you've gathered pointing to something negative?

4. . . . *if you're the only person he's dating.* Do you have any concerns that he's seeing someone else or is unsure of his feelings for you? It may not be official yet, but has he given any indication that he wants to be exclusive with you?

5. . . . *if you really like him beyond a physical attraction.* Do you feel a strong connection beyond the butterflies in your tummy when you see him? Do you enjoy talking to him and going out together, or are you preoccupied with images of what you want him to do to you in bed?

6. . . . *if you can see yourself with him in the long term.* Do you think you'll be with him in three months? Six months? One year? Is there any reason why you wouldn't see yourself with him in the long term?

7. . . . *what your ex is doing.* Are you still thinking about your ex-boyfriend? Do you still ask mutual friends about him or Google him? Do you secretly hope that someday you two will get back together?

8. . . . *if your lifestyles are compatible.* Do you enjoy spending time together? Do you have the same priorities when it comes to making time for relationships? Do you have a similar vision of the future?

9. . . . *if you should take down your online-dating profile.* Are you unsure whether you're ready to give up corresponding with all those guys online? Are you still curious about the other men you may meet? Do you feel like you want to leave your profile up "just in case"?

10. *. . . what you would do if that really cute guy at work finally asked for your number.* Are there still guys out there who you'd choose over this one? Do you secretly hope one of them will make a move? Do you think you would be receptive, or do you picture yourself saying, "Sorry, but I have a boyfriend"?

If you've truly stopped wondering, congratulations! You're ready for a committed relationship! But how do you know if *he's* ready to commit? Carefully think about these questions regarding *his* signals:

1. *Does he feel that you fit into his life?* Has he taken you out with his friends? Does he talk about taking you to work functions? Do his friends and/or family members tell you that he talks about you a lot?

2. *Does he feel good with you on his arm?* Is he comfortable holding your hand or giving you a kiss in public?

3. *Is he willing to wait to have sex? Does he respect your desire to slowly pace the relationship?* Does he seem intrigued or annoyed by waiting to become intimate?

4. *Does he feel that there's someone better out there for him?* Is he still looking? Does he check out other women when he's out with you? Has he taken down *his* online profile?

5. *Is he making you a priority in his life?* Does he have trouble deciding if he should go out with you or the guys on Saturday night? Does he frequently cancel plans with you?

6. *Is he willing to spend money on something nice for you?* Is he generous? Is it easy for him to do something thoughtful?

7. *Is he attracted to you?* Does he compliment how you look? Does he look his best for you?

8. *Can he see himself with you in the long term?* Does he talk about the future? Has he asked you to be his girlfriend?

9. *Does he enjoy your company when you're not naked?* Is he interested in getting to know you? Does he seem engaged when you're talking and interested in what you have to say? Do your conversations always seem to move to sexual topics?

10. *Does he care about you?* Does he respect your opinion and ask for your advice when he has a problem? Does he make sure that you're safe and comfortable? Is he considerate of your feelings?

By the end of three months, you should be able to answer these questions and know if you're both ready for a committed, lasting relationship. At this point, you'll be even more certain that you want to be together even though you're not rushing toward an engagement ring. You've successfully planted this seed in your romance garden, and it's ready to bloom!

You're Ready to Commit—Now What?

The time has come to commit without having that awkward "State of the Union" talk. You've communicated your interest and have already established the fact that you desire a fulfilling relationship. Your emotions are deepening, and you've given the right body-language signals.

By now, he probably also has a sense of moving into the committed stage. No guy is going to wait three months for sex for no good reason! But what if he hasn't said anything by Date #12? As he progresses with the physical moves, you can simply say, "You know how I feel about relationships. For me, sexual intimacy is part of being committed to someone." Most times, you won't even have to say that much.

If, however, he says that he isn't interested in a committed relationship but still wants to see you, then *stop*. Is this what you really want? Our advice is for you to move on and don't look back. It's clear that you want different things, and this is obviously not the greatest man for you. You want a great guy who wants to have a great *relationship with you*. If this happens, have *faith* that your ideal mate is still out there . . . *because he is!* It *is* possible!

Please don't try to change a guy's mind. A guy isn't going to suddenly change his mind because you put in more time and effort. If you think expressing your feelings will help, he'll run for the hills. He's communicated a strong message: He likes "hanging out" with you but is focused on other things.

On the flip side, however, he may say, "Will you be my girlfriend?" Once again, the SW Method has worked! And you will wonder no more.

How to Break Off with Other Guys after Committing

When you make a commitment, you inevitably have to say good-bye to the other men you've been dating. How do you do this in the best possible way? Well, you should say something like: "Tom, you know I've been going on dates with some other guys. It turns out that I have a stronger connection with one of them. You're a great guy, and obviously, we get along really well, but it's not a match for me."

Do this in a formal way in person or on the phone. Do *not* break it off with someone via e-mail or text message. Do you remember the episode of *Sex and the City* when Carrie's boyfriend Berger broke up with her on a Post-it note? She was left feeling rejected and wondering what went wrong. Don't do that to

someone; instead, be clear and don't put it off. Don't offer hope for the future or be cruel and play with a person's emotions. Just say, "This isn't going to work out for me."

He might reply with, "Can I still call you?" Perhaps you can still be friends, but this doesn't usually work for most because the guy you are *breaking off* with may still be interested in dating you. For him, being your friend may just be his way of staying close so that he can make a move in the future. We advise you to make a clean break.

I (Dr. C) want to warn you that sometimes women keep a string of men around who are interested in them because they like the attention. They're less interested in developing friendships and more into the ego boost that comes from *pseudo-dating* a guy—going to dinner or a movie and allowing men to pursue them without the emotional risk of actually dating. These women may be doing this because they're insecure and wish to avoid authentic relationships.

However, if a genuine friendship develops out of a seed that doesn't grow in your romance garden, that's wonderful.

Cultivating Your First Bloom

Should you end your membership on online-dating sites? Many women will check to see if their new mate is still logging on to Internet dating sites. We think there's no reason to visit dating sites unless you're holding out for something better. If you're in a new relationship, don't freak out and go on the attack if you see your new boyfriend's profile on a site. Relationships are all about communication, so you should clearly explain your concerns.

For example, you can say, "For me, having a commitment is just about the two of us. If you're still cruising online-dating sites, it makes me a little uncomfortable. Can we talk about it?" On the other hand, what if he wants to remain great friends with his ex but you suspect that she's interested in getting back together with him? How do you keep things passionate a year into the relationship? Oh my—you're about to meet his mother. . . .

Stop fueling your MFDA, and pull those weeds! Even though you've entered a committed relationship, it's vital that you continue tending your garden. Cultivating the seven factors will increase your overall happiness (by creating a positive mind-set) and will greatly enhance your romance.

We truly hope we've helped take the confusion out of the dating process for good, offering you the tools you need to feel empowered in the modern dating scene. Tune in to your inner wisdom and passion, and grow the fulfilling love life you desire and deserve. Enjoy cultivating your seeds!

Epilogue

If you're about to say, "Well, it may never happen to me," we have one last bit of advice: *Stop wondering if you'll ever meet him!*

We mean it—*seriously.*

Stop it right now! You *will* meet him, and when that happens, you'll know exactly what to do. Your seed is waiting for you as you read this, so please keep the faith and get out there.

Until next time . . .

Ryan and Dr. C

Acknowledgments

Ryan and Dr. C would like to thank:

Louise Hay, whose vision inspired us to seek out her publishing company. Just to be mentioned in the same breath as Louise and the countless talented authors in the Hay House family is amazing. Reid Tracy, for not only believing in us enough to give us a chance, but also for taking us under his wing and showing us the ropes along the way. Jill Kramer, for her wisdom, humor, patience, and joyful spirit. Lisa Mitchell, for her precise editorial comments and confidence in us. Amy Rose Grigoriou, for her spectacular cover, unbounded creativity, and artistic contribution to our vision. A special thanks to the other team members at Hay House, including Stacey Smith, Margarete Nielsen, Christy Salinas, Jeannie Liberati, John Thompson, Jacqui Clark, Carina Sammartino, Lindsay Condict, Summer McStravick, Kyle Rector, and Patrick Gabrysiak. Your enthusiasm and support mean so much to us. To everyone else at Hay House who worked on this project without our direct knowledge, thank you.

Our gratitude also goes to Cindy Pearlman, who helped us carve a beautiful sculpture from a mass of information that would have overwhelmed many. You guided our voices into this wonderful book, and we couldn't have done it without you. Thank you to Josh, for your business sense, ingenious marketing strategies, and hilarious dating tips. Anthony, for your support and endless confidence in this project. Honoree, for your incredible coaching and encouragement. Paul, for your generous guidance and vast knowledge about every conceivable subject. Andy, Bobie, Damon, Elyse, Rose, Sean, and Scott, for your friendship and support.

To all of our clients and students over the years, thank you for trusting us with the most intimate parts of your lives—without you, we would have never been able to refine this system and write this book.

Wondering . . .

Ryan would like to thank:

Dad, for your guidance and assistance over the years, and for encouraging me to find my vision and have confidence in myself. Mom, for always supporting and believing in me throughout my many twists and turns in life. Tyler, who inspires me to be my best; and my three younger siblings, Samantha, Jordan, and Zach, who have always understood me deeply and loved me enough to listen to my years of unsolicited advice. To my Rimpa, Roger Davis, for supporting me over the years with everything I needed. Laura, thanks for all the understanding; I love you, and your love for my grandfather is magical. To Tim, Lori, Jeff, Monda, Christie, Gil, and Ronny, I love you all dearly. Surf that wave, Ronny, then paint it into your perfect sunset. You are always with me.

To any (and most likely, all) girlfriends and exes whom I caused emotional pain as a result of my unclear sexual behavior and immature communication, I'm sorry. I have you to thank for the countless lessons I've learned over the years. I made mistakes because I didn't know what I was doing, but because of our experiences together, I set out on my journey to write this book. Thank you, and I love you all for your teachings. To my guy friends: I learned with you as we chased skirts and broke hearts. You know who you are; between us, we've shared a lifetime of experiences, and many more lie ahead. To my female friends, thank you for letting me practice coaching you over the years. A special thanks to Heather for your belief in me, and Kelly for your unique style and friendship over the years.

And to Jessica, from the first time we met, you deeply impacted my life. I'll never forget those first encounters in psychology class where we challenged each other, holding one another to high standards of personal excellence. I knew then, in those moments, that we would be business partners forever and that we'd do great things together. You were my guide and friend, a trusted ally and adviser. I love you with all my heart—always have. I just didn't know that it was *romantic love,* which is what it turned out to be. And for that, I am blessed.

Dr. C would also like to thank:

Ken Browning, for your astute guidance and dedication to this project. Mom and Dad, for your loving support, patience, and endless encouragement. My brother, Dan, for your support (and humor) as you listened to all of your big sister's brilliant ideas. Grandma Frances, for inspiring, supporting, and encouraging me through this process. Gina and Aaron, for always supporting me and being great friends. Oscar, my person of honor, for your friendship and guidance. Tara, for helping me explore my artistic side. Ali, for your friendship, support, and of course, the shenanigans. Ellen, for your friendship, guidance, and wonderful memories of Samoa. Jennifer, for your friendship and our memories of NYC. Dreyfus, for your love, companionship, and strength; you taught me to never give up.

To all of my wonderful friends and family, who've contributed to my personal and professional development by teaching, inspiring, and supporting me through the years. To all of my exes, great romances, and horrible dates; these experiences taught me about life, love, and relationships.

To Ryan, my collaborator, my best friend, and my love. Thank you for showing me that it's all possible! You've taught me more about love and relationships than I ever hoped to learn. From the moment we met, I knew that we had something special. I just never imagined that our successful partnership would become a great romantic relationship. Thank you for being courageous and reminding me that together, we can do anything.

About the Authors

Ryan Browning Cassaday is a certified life coach who has received extensive training at the advanced level. He runs a worldwide dating and relationship consulting practice with his new wife, Jessica Cassaday, Ph.D.; and has co-created a revolutionary approach to dating and relationships called the Stop Wondering Method. Jessica and Ryan met eight years ago in graduate school and fell in love while writing this book. It just added further proof that their SW Method works.

A California native, Ryan always wanted to help people have more meaningful and complete relationships with each other. He's had a lifelong interest in developing a deep understanding of psychological growth and motivation, and has a B.S. in psychology from Union College with a special emphasis on developmental psychology.

Ryan began his career by working with children of all ages and backgrounds, dealing with everything from increasing self-esteem to healing the wounds of divorce. He's helped kids as young as four years old through young adults, as well as their parents. From classrooms to camping trips, he'd work with the entire family in order to create solid bonds and help individuals reclaim their self-worth while finding a new direction in life. In his spare time, Ryan also had an extremely successful career as an actor and worked on stage, TV, and film.

At a certain point, Ryan had to make the decision as to whether he wanted to act or work as a life coach because his time was becoming limited. So he took a step back from acting to pursue his true passion. His mission has always been to help people live more fulfilling lives.

Ryan has taken his experience as an actor and has effortlessly applied those skills to his work as a coach and speaker. *Stop Wondering If You'll Ever Meet Him* is his first book. He's about to embark on a nationwide seminar tour on dating and relationships and is the co-founder of **EWONDERDATES.com**, an exciting, new Website. In addition, he's the host of a syndicated radio show with Dr. C, which airs on **HayHouseRadio.com.**

Website: **www.stopwonderingbook.com**

Jessica Cassaday, Ph.D., also known as Dr. C, is a clinical psychologist from New York who runs a successful relationship and dating consulting practice with her new husband, Ryan Browning Cassaday. Together they consult with clients all over the world on dating, love, sex, and relationship issues. Her personal passion for helping people have better relationships, combined with advanced training in sex therapy, has led to the creation of a unique and innovative approach to dating and relationships called the Stop Wondering Method.

A native of Long Island, New York, she has treated individuals all over the world who have a wide range of complex psychological issues. She has also led countless groups, including many focused on sexuality and safer-sex practices, as well as support groups for women. As Associate Director of Research of the Los Angeles Sexuality Center, she presented research at the annual American Association of Sex Educators, Counselors, and Therapists (AASECT) conference and worked on a documentary that was shown at the World Congress of Sexology in Havana, Cuba.

Dr. C has provided clinical supervision and training for psychology graduate students and has lectured in the United States and Europe. She is a gifted teacher and mentor, and captivates audiences with her on-target insights.

She's about to embark on a nationwide seminar tour on dating and relationships and is the co-founder of **EWONDERDATES. com,** an exciting, new Website. She's also the host of a syndicated radio show with Ryan Browning Cassaday, which airs on **Hay HouseRadio.com.**

Website: **www.stopwonderingbook.com**

notes

notes

notes

We hope you enjoyed this Hay House book. If you'd like
to receive a free catalog featuring additional Hay House books
and products, or if you'd like information about the
Hay Foundation, please contact:

Hay House, Inc.
P.O. Box 5100
Carlsbad, CA 92018-5100

(760) 431-7695 or **(800) 654-5126**
(760) 431-6948 (fax) or **(800) 650-5115 (fax)**
www.hayhouse.com® • **www.hayfoundation.org**

Published and distributed in Australia by:
Hay House Australia Pty. Ltd., 18/36 Ralph St., Alexandria NSW 2015
Phone: 612-9669-4299 • *Fax:* 612-9669-4144 • www.hayhouse.com.au

Published and distributed in the United Kingdom by:
Hay House UK, Ltd., 292B Kensal Rd., London W10 5BE • *Phone:*
44-20-8962-1230 • *Fax:* 44-20-8962-1239 • www.hayhouse.co.uk

Published and distributed in the Republic of South Africa by:
Hay House SA (Pty), Ltd., P.O. Box 990, Witkoppen 2068 • *Phone/Fax:*
27-11-467-8904 • orders@psdprom.co.za • www.hayhouse.co.za

Published in India by: Hay House Publishers India, Muskaan
Complex, Plot No. 3, B-2, Vasant Kunj, New Delhi 110 070 • *Phone:*
91-11-4176-1620 • *Fax:* 91-11-4176-1630 • www.hayhouse.co.in

Distributed in Canada by: Raincoast, 9050 Shaughnessy St.,
Vancouver, B.C. V6P 6E5 • *Phone:* (604) 323-7100
Fax: (604) 323-2600 • www.raincoast.com

Tune in to **HayHouseRadio.com®** for the best in inspirational
talk radio featuring top Hay House authors! And, sign up via the
Hay House USA Website to receive the Hay House online newsletter
and stay informed about what's going on with your favorite authors.
You'll receive bimonthly announcements about Discounts
and Offers, Special Events, Product Highlights,
Free Excerpts, Giveaways, and more!
www.hayhouse.com®